THIS BOOK WAS GIFTED BY
IAIN MACNEIL, MANAGING DIRECTOR
WITHERBY SEAMANSHIP INTERNATIONAL.
15:07:12.

M. M____

MASTER.

ENC Chart 1 Symbol Guide

By: ECDIS Ltd

ECDIS
limited

First edition published 2012

ISBN: 978-1-85609-547-1

© ECDIS Ltd, 2012

British Library Cataloguing in Publication Data
A catalogue record for this book is available from the British Library.

Printed and bound in Great Britain by Bell & Bain Ltd, Glasgow

Published by

Witherby Publishing Group Ltd
4 Dunlop Square, Livingston
Edinburgh, EH54 8SB
Scotland, UK

Tel No: +44(0)1506 463 227
Fax No: +44(0)1506 468 999

Email: info@emailws.com
Web: www.witherbys.com

ECDIS Chart 1 Index

Chart 1 Index including Mariners' Navigational Symbols

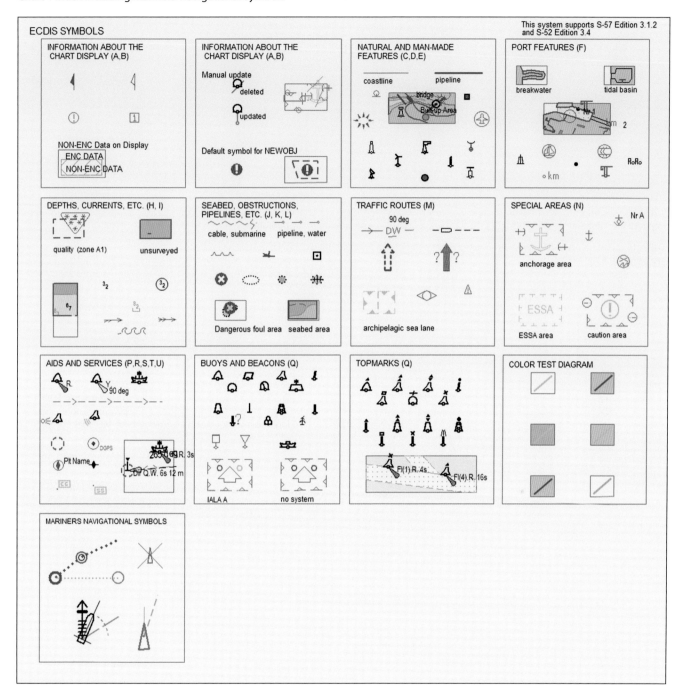

Note that the printed version of Mariner' Navigational Symbols is included in this document for reasons of completeness. Because IEC 62288 [3] is the ruling standard for these symbols, the cell AAC1XMS.000 containing Mariner' Navigational Symbols as special objects is no longer included in the S-52, Appendix 2 package.

ECDIS Chart 1 Index excluding Mariners' Navigational Symbols

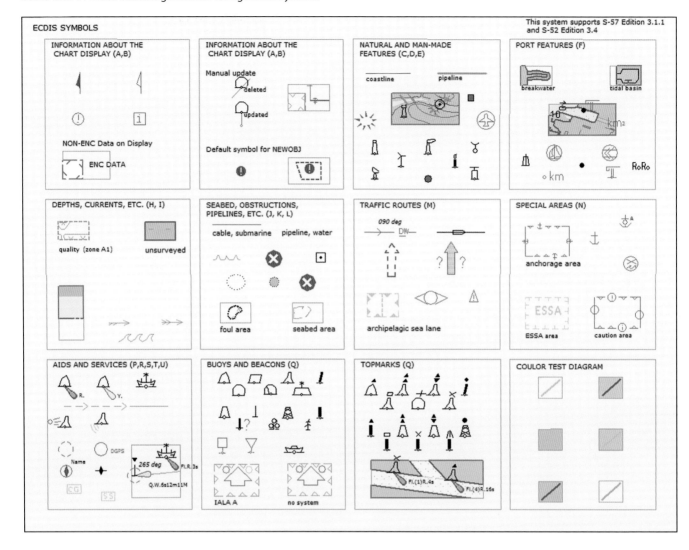

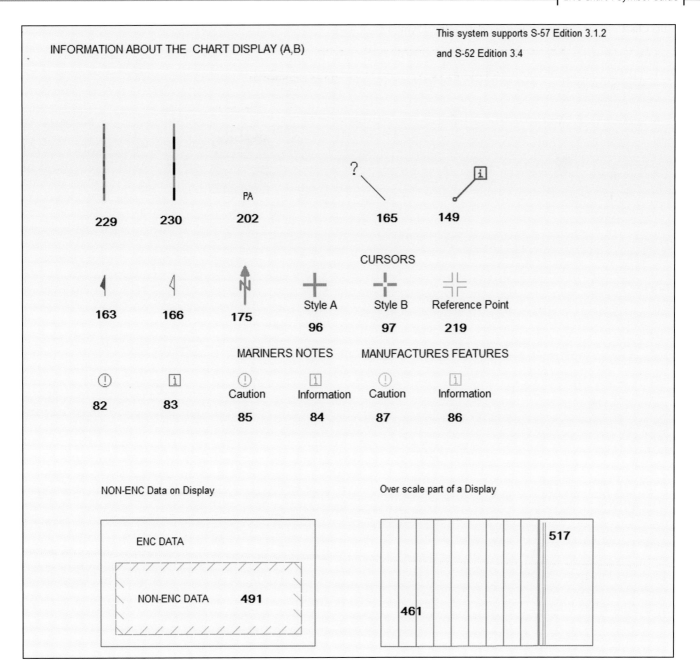

INFORMATION ABOUT THE CHART DISPLAY (A,B)

This system supports S-57 Edition 3.1.2

and S-52 Edition 3.4

229   230   202   165   149

PA

CURSORS

163   166   175   Style A   Style B   Reference Point

96   97   219

MARINERS NOTES   MANUFACTURES FEATURES

82   83   Caution   Information   Caution   Information

85   84   87   86

NON-ENC Data on Display   Over scale part of a Display

ENC DATA   517

NON-ENC DATA   491

461

INFORMATION ABOUT THE CHART DISPLAY (A,B)

This system supports S-57 Edition 3.1.2 and S-52 Edition 3.4

Test symbol for size checking

Test symbol for color checking

■ **88**

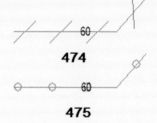

523

Manual update

🜨 deleted
78

🜨 updated
79

⊸ 60 ⊸
474

⊸ 60 ⊸
475

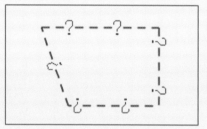

No symbol exists in the symbol library

?
204

- -?- - -?- - -?- -
505

Default symbol for NEWOBJ

❶
585

❶- -❶- -❶- -❶- -
588

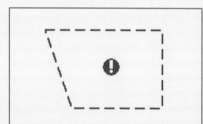

NATURAL AND MAN-MADE FEATURES (C,D,E)

This system supports S-57 Edition 3.1.2
and S-52 Edition 3.4

coastline, surveyed

land elevation

pipeline, overhead

coastline, unsurveyed

vegetation

cable, overhead

river, stream

road

fixed bridge

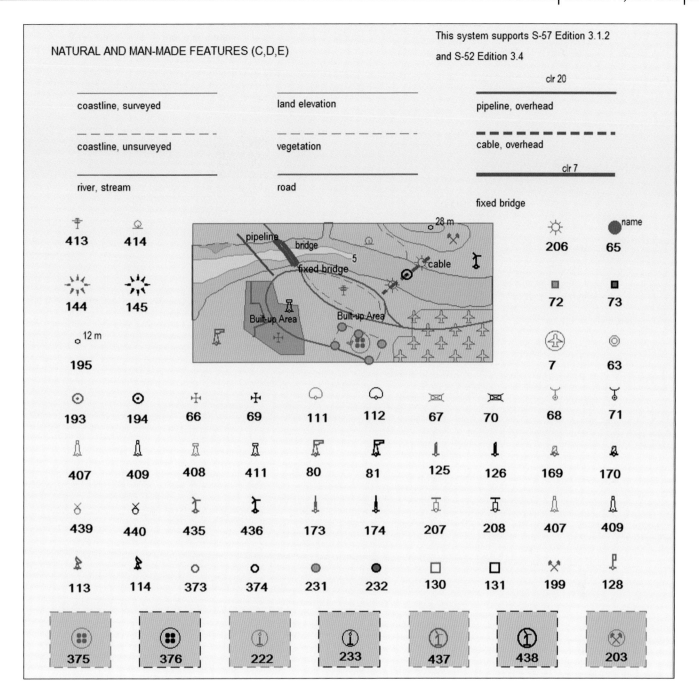

413	414							206	65
144	145							72	73
195								7	63
193	194	66	69	111	112	67	70	68	71
407	409	408	411	80	81	125	126	169	170
439	440	435	436	173	174	207	208	407	409
113	114	373	374	231	232	130	131	199	128
375	376	222	233	437	438				203

PORT FEATURES (F)

This system supports S-57 Edition 3.1.2
and S-52 Edition 3.4

shorline construction	lock gate	dam
breakwater	tidal basin	timber yard

146	234	64 Nr 1	142	143
171	172	188	147	RoRo 234
km 109	∘km 108	♯ 372	179	90

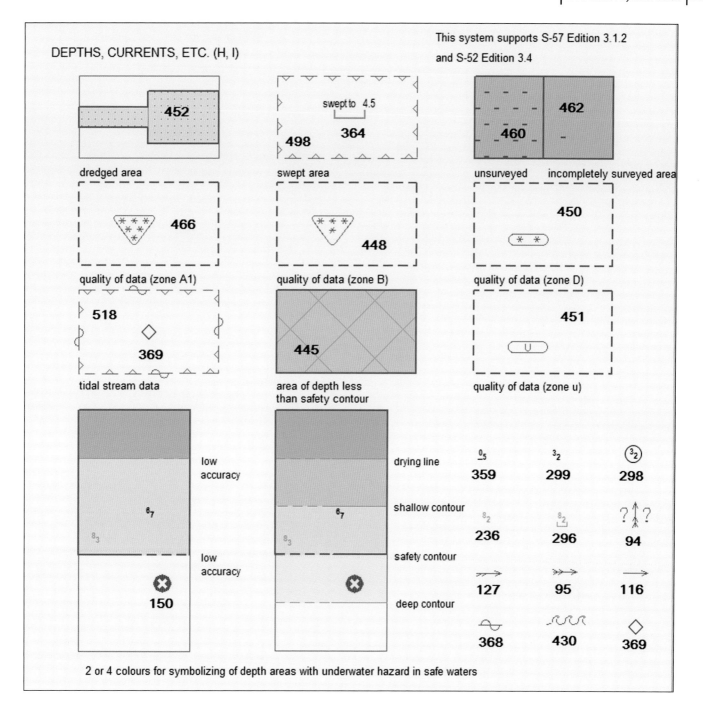

DEPTHS, CURRENTS, ETC. (H, I)

This system supports S-57 Edition 3.1.2 and S-52 Edition 3.4

dredged area

swept area

unsurveyed   incompletely surveyed area

quality of data (zone A1)

quality of data (zone B)

quality of data (zone D)

tidal stream data

area of depth less than safety contour

quality of data (zone u)

low accuracy

drying line

shallow contour

low accuracy

safety contour

deep contour

2 or 4 colours for symbolizing of depth areas with underwater hazard in safe waters

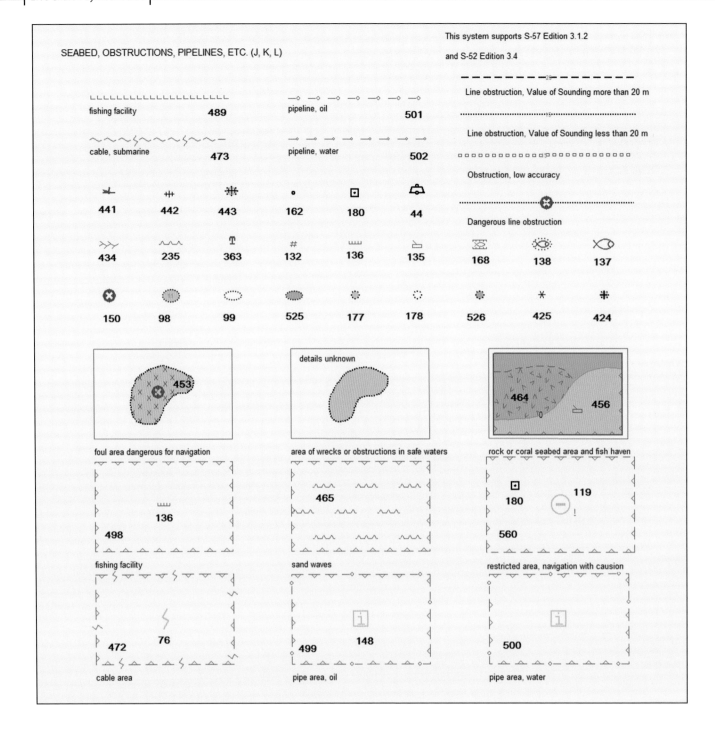

SEABED, OBSTRUCTIONS, PIPELINES, ETC. (J, K, L)

This system supports S-57 Edition 3.1.2

and S-52 Edition 3.4

fishing facility **489**

pipeline, oil **501**

Line obstruction, Value of Sounding more than 20 m

cable, submarine **473**

pipeline, water **502**

Line obstruction, Value of Sounding less than 20 m

Obstruction, low accuracy

441 **442** **443** **162** **180** **44**

Dangerous line obstruction

434 **235** **363** **132** **136** **135** **168** **138** **137**

150 **98** **99** **525** **177** **178** **526** **425** **424**

foul area dangerous for navigation

453

details unknown

rock or coral seabed area and fish haven

464 **456**

fishing facility

136

498

area of wrecks or obstructions in safe waters

465

180 **119**

560

472 **76**

cable area

sand waves

148

499

pipe area, oil

restricted area, navigation with causion

500

pipe area, water

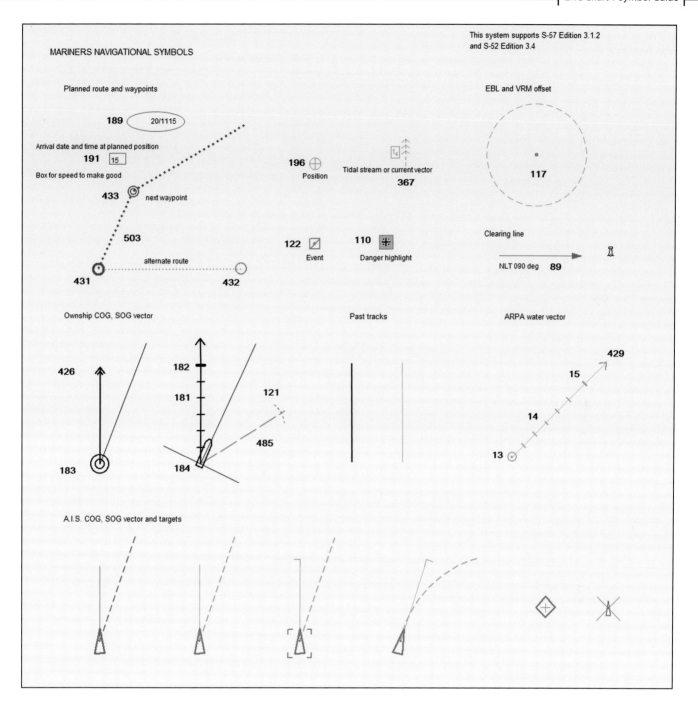

MARINERS NAVIGATIONAL SYMBOLS

This system supports S-57 Edition 3.1.2
and S-52 Edition 3.4

Planned route and waypoints

189   20/1115

Arrival date and time at planned position
191   15

Box for speed to make good

433   next waypoint

503

431   alternate route   432

196   Position

367   Tidal stream or current vector

122   Event

110   Danger highlight

EBL and VRM offset

117

Clearing line

NLT 090 deg   89

Ownship COG, SOG vector

426

183

182

181

184

121

485

Past tracks

ARPA water vector

429

15

14

13

A.I.S. COG, SOG vector and targets

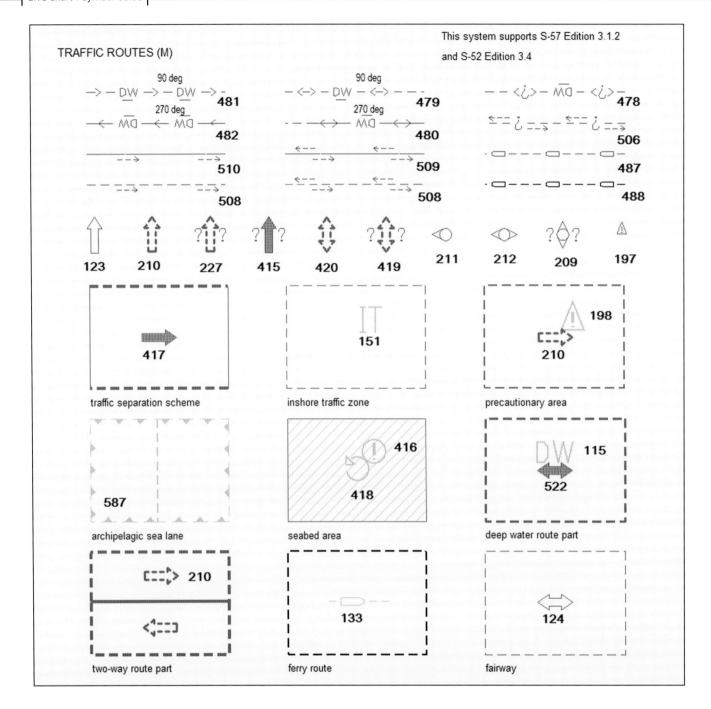

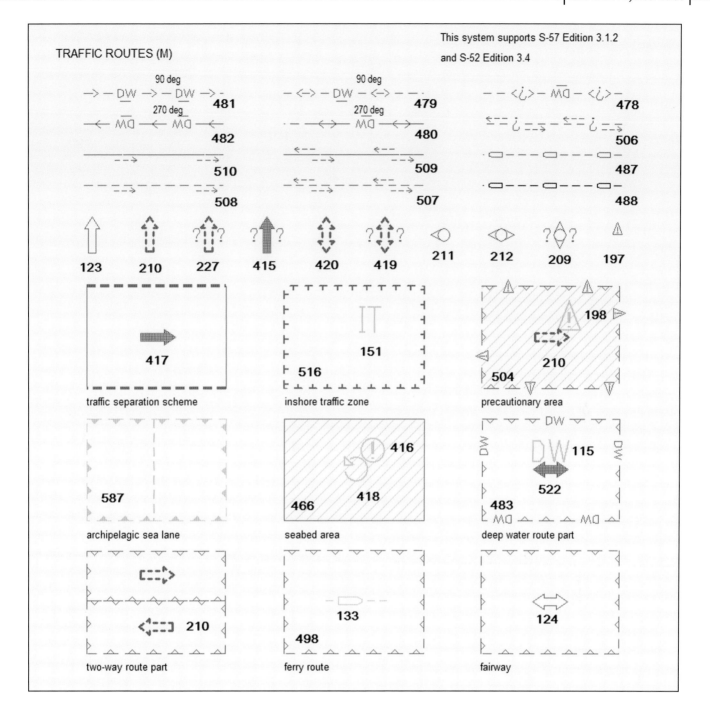

TRAFFIC ROUTES (M)

This system supports S-57 Edition 3.1.2 and S-52 Edition 3.4

traffic separation scheme

inshore traffic zone

precautionary area

archipelagic sea lane

seabed area

deep water route part

two-way route part

ferry route

fairway

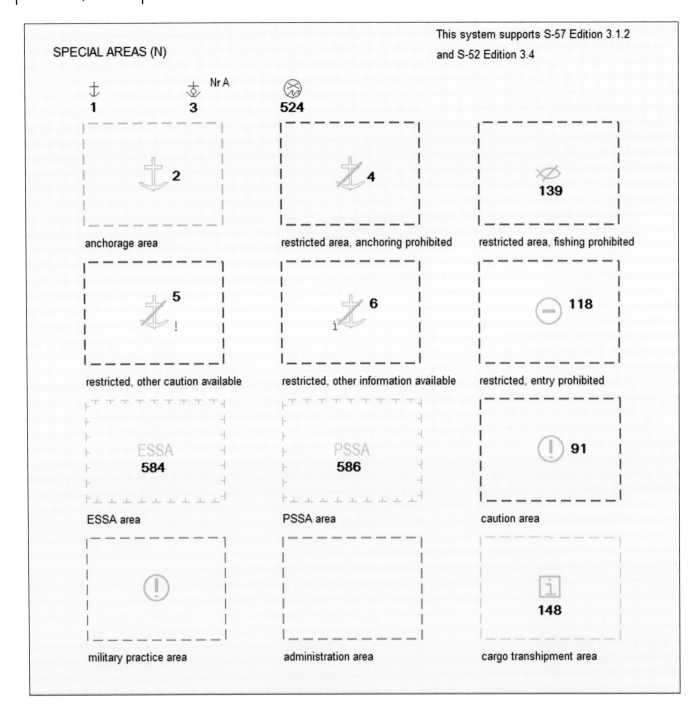

SPECIAL AREAS (N)

This system supports S-57 Edition 3.1.2
and S-52 Edition 3.4

anchorage area

restricted area, anchoring prohibited

restricted area, fishing prohibited

restricted, other caution available

restricted, other information available

restricted, entry prohibited

ESSA area

PSSA area

caution area

military practice area

administration area

cargo transhipment area

SPECIAL AREAS (N)

This system supports S-57 Edition 3.1.2 and S-52 Edition 3.4

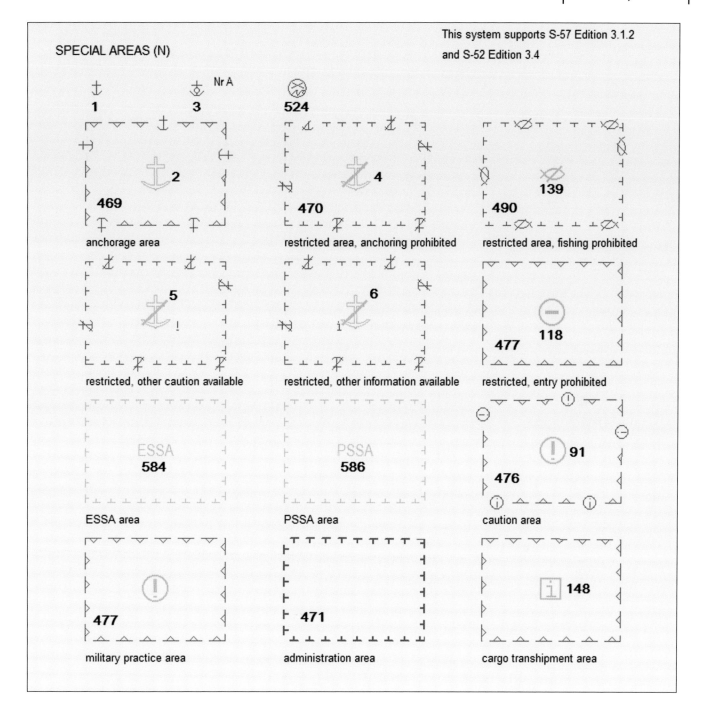

anchorage area	restricted area, anchoring prohibited	restricted area, fishing prohibited
restricted, other caution available	restricted, other information available	restricted, entry prohibited
ESSA area	PSSA area	caution area
military practice area	administration area	cargo transhipment area

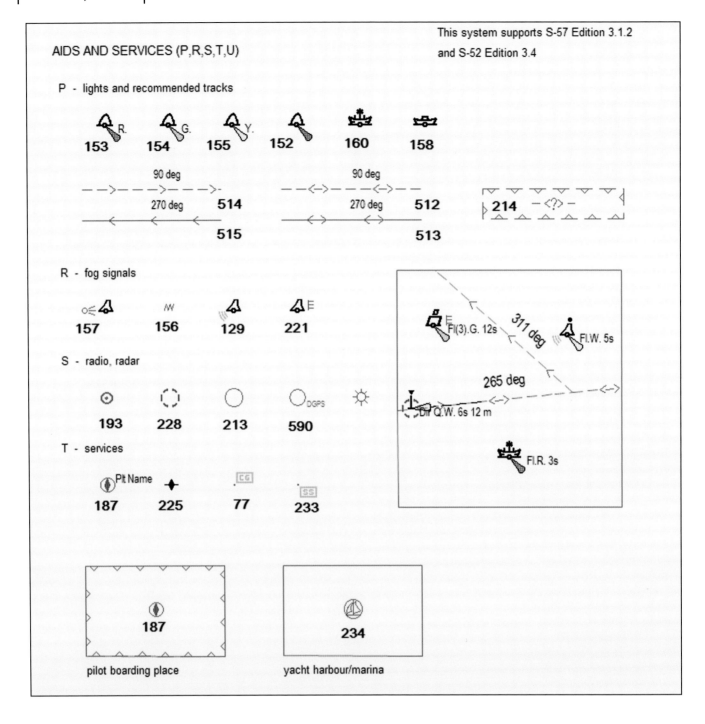

AIDS AND SERVICES (P,R,S,T,U)

This system supports S-57 Edition 3.1.2
and S-52 Edition 3.4

P - lights and recommended tracks

153   154   155   152   160   158

90 deg   514
270 deg
515

90 deg   512
270 deg
513

214

R - fog signals

157   156   129   221

S - radio, radar

193   228   213   590

T - services

Plt Name
187   225   77   233

pilot boarding place

187

yacht harbour/marina

234

Fl(3).G. 12s   311 deg   Fl.W. 5s

265 deg

Dir Q.W. 6s 12 m

Fl.R. 3s

BUOYS AND BEACONS (Q)

This system supports S-57 Edition 3.1.2
and S-52 Edition 3.4

Buoys

41		36		53	59			43
55	35				60	62	50	51

Beacons

34		33		28				22
21				74	75	176	200	201

Daymarks

101   104   105

Light float and light vessel

160   158

Navigational system of marks

A — B — A — B — A — B — A — B — A —
497
B — A — B — A — B — A — B — A — B

106
498

IALA A

107

IALA B

521

no or other system

15

BUOYS AND BEACONS (Q)

This system supports S-57 Edition 3.1.2

and S-52 Edition 3.4

Buoys

46	47	48	49	37	38	39	40	42

45	54	56	57	58	527	61	52	

Beacons

24	25	26	27	16	17	18	19	20

23	29	31	32	74	75	176		

Daymarks

100	102	103

Light float and light vessel

161	159

Navigational system of marks

```
A--B--A--B--A--B--A--B--A--oo
  497
B--A--B--A--B--A--B--A--B--A
```

106	107	521
IALA A	IALA B	no or other system

TOPMARKS (Q)

This system supports S-57 Edition 3.1.2
and S-52 Edition 3.4

Buoys Topmarks

377	378	379	380	381	382	383	384
385	386	387	388	389	401	371	

Beacon topmarks

390	391	392	393	394	395	396	397
398	399	400	402	405	404	406	403

Fl(2).G.8s
Fl(2).R.8s
Fl(2).W.10s
Fl(1).R.4s
Q(3).W.10s
Fl(4).R.16s
Fl(1).G.3s
Fl(4).G.12s

COLOR TEST DIAGRAM

This system supports S-57 Edition 3.1.2
and S-52 Edition 3.4

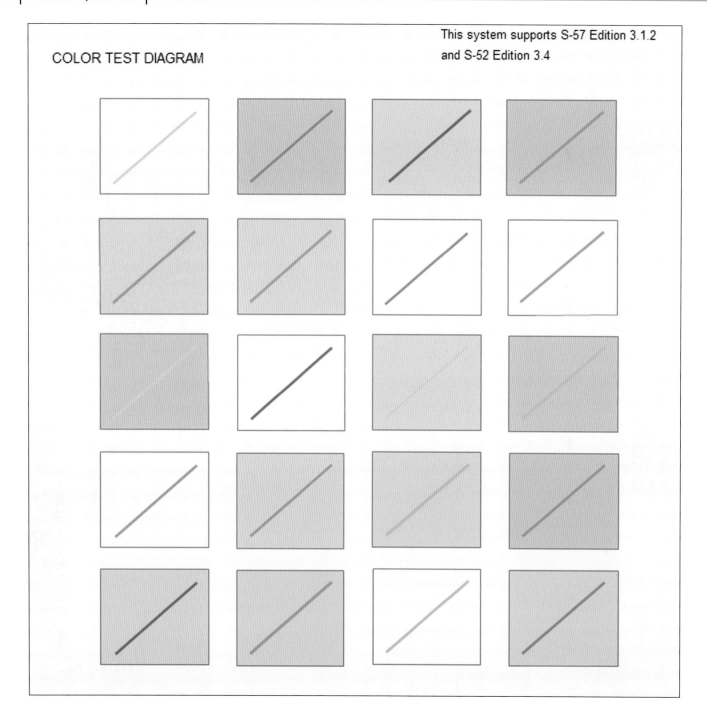

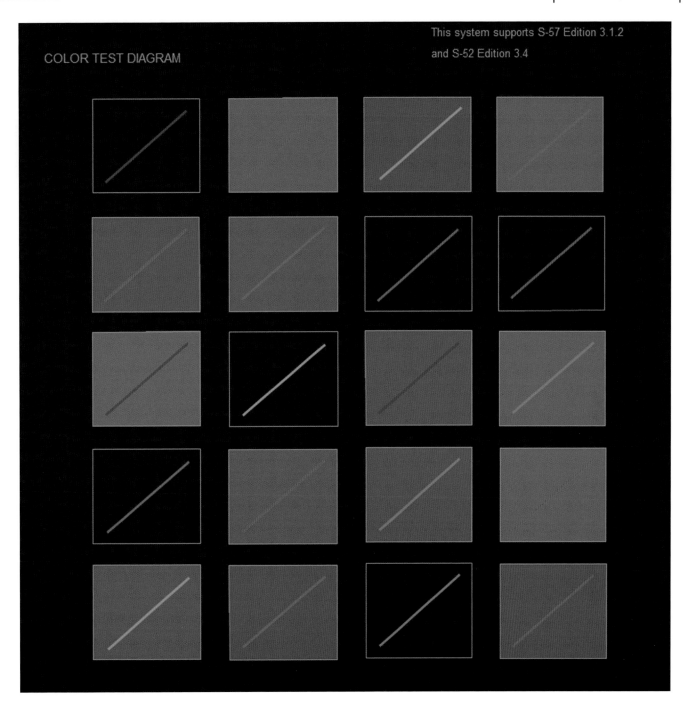

Note that this depiction of selected ECDIS Mariner's Navigational Symbols are included in these specifications for convenience of reference, by courtesy of IEC, who are the authority for them under IEC 62288. The digital version of Chart 1 does no longer include the cell AAC1XMS.000 which presented the above symbols as collected here in preceeding versions of the Presentation Library.

ECDIS Chart 1 Numerical Description List

	Symbol Name:	SY(**ACHARE02**)
	Symbol Number:	1
	Symbol Explanation:	Anchorage area as a point at small scale, or anchor points of mooring trot at large scale
	S57/INT1:	ACHARE N 10, N 12.1-9 (N 10)
		OBSTRN Q 42
	Symbol Name:	SY(**ACHARE51**)
	Symbol Number:	2
	Symbol Explanation:	Anchorage area
	S57/INT1:	ACHARE (centred symbol) N 12.1-9 (N 12.1)
	Symbol Name:	SY(**ACHBRT07**)
	Symbol Number:	3
	Symbol Explanation:	Designated anchor berth for a single vessel
	S57/INT1:	ACHBRT N 11.1, 11.2 (N 11.1)
	Symbol Name:	SY(**ACHRES51**)
	Symbol Number:	4
	Symbol Explanation:	Area where anchoring is prohibited or restricted
	S57/INT1:	RESARE N 20
	Symbol Name:	SY(**ACHRES61**)
	Symbol Number:	5
	Symbol Explanation:	Area where anchoring is prohibited or restricted, with other cautions
	S57/INT1:	RESARE N 20
	Symbol Name:	SY(**ACHRES71**)
	Symbol Number:	6
	Symbol Explanation:	Area where anchoring is prohibited or restricted, with other information
	S57/INT1:	RESARE N 20
	Symbol Name:	SY(**AIRARE02**)
	Symbol Number:	7
	Symbol Explanation:	Symbol for airport as a point
	S57/INT1:	AIRARE D 17
	Symbol Name:	SY(**AISSLP02**)
	Symbol Number:	11
	Symbol Explanation:	Sleeping AIS target
	S57/INT1:	N/A
	Symbol Name:	SY(**AISVES02**)
	Symbol Number:	12
	Symbol Explanation:	Active AIS target showing vector and/or heading
	S57/INT1:	

Symbol Name:	SY(**ARPATG02**)
Symbol Number:	**13**
Symbol Explanation:	ARPA target
S57/INT1:	N/A

Symbol Name:	SY(**ARPONE02**)
Symbol Number:	**14**
Symbol Explanation:	One minute mark on ARPA vector
S57/INT1:	N/A

Symbol Name:	SY(**ARPSIX02**)
Symbol Number:	**15**
Symbol Explanation:	Six minute mark on ARPA vector
S57/INT1:	N/A

Symbol Name:	SY(**BCNCAR01**)
Symbol Number:	**16**
Symbol Explanation:	Cardinal beacon, north, simplified
S57/INT1:	BCNCAR Q 130.3

Symbol Name:	SY(**BCNCAR02**)
Symbol Number:	**17**
Symbol Explanation:	Cardinal beacon, east, simplified
S57/INT1:	BCNCAR Q 130.3

Symbol Name:	SY(**BCNCAR03**)
Symbol Number:	**18**
Symbol Explanation:	Cardinal beacon, south, simplified
S57/INT1:	BCNCAR Q 130.3

Symbol Name:	SY(**BCNCAR04**)
Symbol Number:	**19**
Symbol Explanation:	Cardinal beacon, west, simplified
S57/INT1:	BCNCAR Q 130.3

Symbol Name:	SY(**BCNDEF13**)
Symbol Number:	**20**
Symbol Explanation:	Default symbol for a beacon, simplified
S57/INT1:	BCNCAR Q 130.3
	BCNLAT Q 91-92;130.1
	BCNSPP Q 120-125; 130.6
	BCNISD Q 130.4
	BCNSAW Q 130.5

Symbol Name:	SY(**BCNGEN01**)
Symbol Number:	**21**
Symbol Explanation:	Beacon in general, paper-chart
S57/INT1:	BCNCAR Q 130.3
	BCNISD Q 130.4
	BCNLAT Q 91-92;130.1
	BCNSAW Q 130.5
	BCNSPP Q 120-125; 130.6

Symbol Name:	SY(**BCNGEN03**)
Symbol Number:	**22**
Symbol Explanation:	Default symbol for beacon, paper-chart
S57/INT1:	BCNCAR Q 130.3
	BCNISD Q 130.4
	BCNLAT Q 91-92;130.1
	BCNSAW Q 130.5
	BCNSPP Q 120-125; 130.6

	Symbol Name:	SY(BCNISD21)
	Symbol Number:	23
	Symbol Explanation:	Isolated danger beacon, simplified
	S57/INT1:	BCNISD Q 83; 130.4

	Symbol Name:	SY(BCNLAT15)
	Symbol Number:	24
	Symbol Explanation:	Major lateral beacon, red, simplified
	S57/INT1:	BCNLAT Q 130.1

	Symbol Name:	SY(BCNLAT16)
	Symbol Number:	25
	Symbol Explanation:	Major lateral beacon, green, simplified
	S57/INT1:	BCNLAT Q 130.1

	Symbol Name:	SY(BCNLAT21)
	Symbol Number:	26
	Symbol Explanation:	Minor lateral beacon, red, simplified
	S57/INT1:	BCNLAT Q 91-92 ;130.1

	Symbol Name:	SY(BCNLAT21)
	Symbol Number:	27
	Symbol Explanation:	Minor lateral beacon, red, simplified
	S57/INT1:	BCNLAT Q 91-92 ;130.1

	Symbol Name:	SY(BCNLTC01)
	Symbol Number:	28
	Symbol Explanation:	Lattice beacon, paper-chart
	S57/INT1:	BCNCAR Q 130.3
		BCNISD Q 130.4
		BCNLAT Q 91-92;130.1
		BCNSAW Q 130.5
		BCNSPP Q 130.6
		BCNxxx Q 111

	Symbol Name:	SY(BCNSAW13)
	Symbol Number:	29
	Symbol Explanation:	Major safe water beacon, simplified
	S57/INT1:	BCNSAW Q 130.5

	Symbol Name:	SY(BCNSAW21)
	Symbol Number:	30
	Symbol Explanation:	Minor safe water beacon, simplified
	S57/INT1:	BCNSAW Q 130.5

	Symbol Name:	SY(BCNSPP13)
	Symbol Number:	31
	Symbol Explanation:	Major special purpose beacon, simplified
	S57/INT1	BCNSPP Q 130.6

	Symbol Name:	SY(BCNSPP21)
	Symbol Number:	32
	Symbol Explanation:	Minor special purpose beacon, simplified
	S57/INT1	BCNSPP Q 130.6

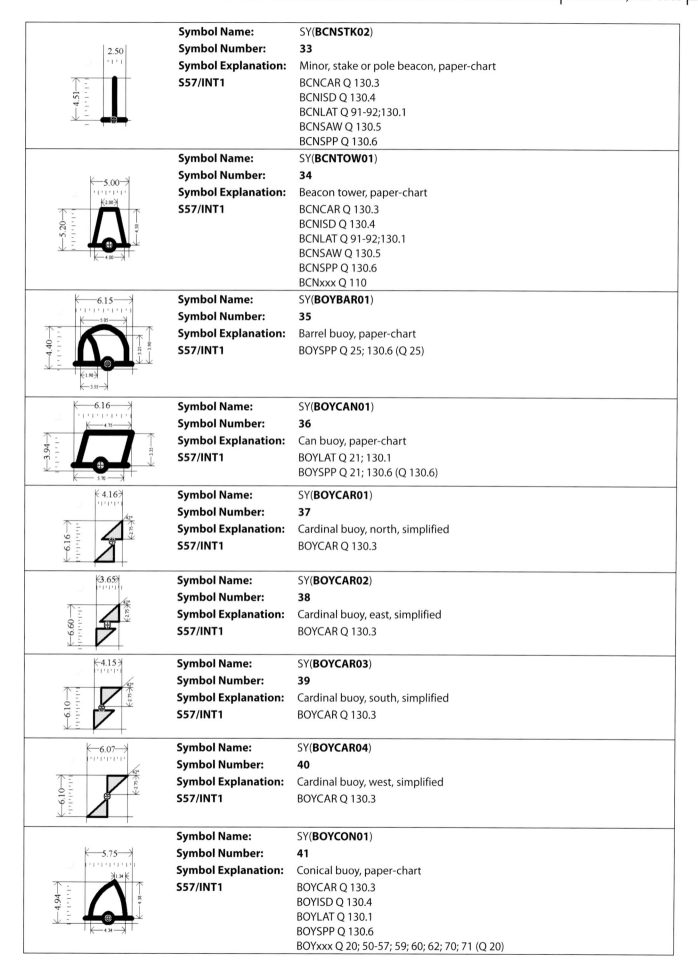

Symbol Name:	SY(**BCNSTK02**)	
Symbol Number:	**33**	
Symbol Explanation:	Minor, stake or pole beacon, paper-chart	
S57/INT1	BCNCAR Q 130.3	
	BCNISD Q 130.4	
	BCNLAT Q 91-92;130.1	
	BCNSAW Q 130.5	
	BCNSPP Q 130.6	

Symbol Name:	SY(**BCNTOW01**)	
Symbol Number:	**34**	
Symbol Explanation:	Beacon tower, paper-chart	
S57/INT1	BCNCAR Q 130.3	
	BCNISD Q 130.4	
	BCNLAT Q 91-92;130.1	
	BCNSAW Q 130.5	
	BCNSPP Q 130.6	
	BCNxxx Q 110	

Symbol Name:	SY(**BOYBAR01**)	
Symbol Number:	**35**	
Symbol Explanation:	Barrel buoy, paper-chart	
S57/INT1	BOYSPP Q 25; 130.6 (Q 25)	

Symbol Name:	SY(**BOYCAN01**)	
Symbol Number:	**36**	
Symbol Explanation:	Can buoy, paper-chart	
S57/INT1	BOYLAT Q 21; 130.1	
	BOYSPP Q 21; 130.6 (Q 130.6)	

Symbol Name:	SY(**BOYCAR01**)	
Symbol Number:	**37**	
Symbol Explanation:	Cardinal buoy, north, simplified	
S57/INT1	BOYCAR Q 130.3	

Symbol Name:	SY(**BOYCAR02**)	
Symbol Number:	**38**	
Symbol Explanation:	Cardinal buoy, east, simplified	
S57/INT1	BOYCAR Q 130.3	

Symbol Name:	SY(**BOYCAR03**)	
Symbol Number:	**39**	
Symbol Explanation:	Cardinal buoy, south, simplified	
S57/INT1	BOYCAR Q 130.3	

Symbol Name:	SY(**BOYCAR04**)	
Symbol Number:	**40**	
Symbol Explanation:	Cardinal buoy, west, simplified	
S57/INT1	BOYCAR Q 130.3	

Symbol Name:	SY(**BOYCON01**)	
Symbol Number:	**41**	
Symbol Explanation:	Conical buoy, paper-chart	
S57/INT1	BOYCAR Q 130.3	
	BOYISD Q 130.4	
	BOYLAT Q 130.1	
	BOYSPP Q 130.6	
	BOYxxx Q 20; 50-57; 59; 60; 62; 70; 71 (Q 20)	

Symbol Name:	SY(**BOYDEF03**)
Symbol Number:	**42**
Symbol Explanation:	Default symbol for buoy, simplified
S57/INT1	BOYCAR Q 130.3
	BOYLAT Q 130.1

Symbol Name:	SY(**BOYGEN03**)
Symbol Number:	**43**
Symbol Explanation:	Default symbol for buoy, paper-chart
S57/INT1	BOYCAR Q 130.3
	BOYISD Q 130.4
	BOYLAT Q 130.1
	BOYSAW Q 130.5
	BOYSPP Q 130.6

Symbol Name:	SY(**BOYINB01**)
Symbol Number:	**44**
Symbol Explanation:	Installation buoy, paper-chart
S57/INT1	BOYINB L 16

Symbol Name:	SY(**BOYISD12**)
Symbol Number:	**45**
Symbol Explanation:	Isolated danger buoy, simplified
S57/INT1	BOYISD Q 130.4

Symbol Name:	SY(**BOYLAT13**)
Symbol Number:	**46**
Symbol Explanation:	Conical lateral buoy, green, simplified
S57/INT1	BOYLAT Q 130.1

Symbol Name:	SY(**BOYLAT14**)
Symbol Number:	**47**
Symbol Explanation:	Conical lateral buoy, red, simplified
S57/INT1	BOYLAT Q 130.1

Symbol Name:	SY(**BOYLAT23**)
Symbol Number:	**48**
Symbol Explanation:	Can shape lateral buoy, green, simplified
S57/INT1	BOYLAT Q 130.1

Symbol Name:	SY(**BOYLAT24**)
Symbol Number:	**49**
Symbol Explanation:	Can shape lateral buoy, red, simplified
S57/INT1	BOYLAT Q 130.1

Symbol Name:	SY(**BOYMOR01**)
Symbol Number:	**50**
Symbol Explanation:	Mooring buoy, barrel shape, paper-chart
S57/INT1	MORFAC Q 40-43 Q 40

Symbol Name:	SY(**BOYMOR03**)
Symbol Number:	**51**
Symbol Explanation:	Mooring buoy, can shape, paper-chart
S57/INT1	MORFAC Q 40-43 Q 40

Symbol Name:	SY(**BOYMOR11**)
Symbol Number:	**52**
Symbol Explanation:	Installation buoy and mooring buoy, simplified
S57/INT1	BOYINB L 16
	MORFAC Q 40-43

Symbol Name:	SY(**BOYPIL01**)
Symbol Number:	**53**
Symbol Explanation:	Pillar buoy, paper-chart
S57/INT1	BOYxxx Q 23
	BOYCAR Q 130.3
	BOYISD Q 130.4
	BOYLAT Q 130.1
	BOYSAW Q 130.5
	BOYSPP Q 130.6

Symbol Name:	SY(**BOYSAW12**)
Symbol Number:	**54**
Symbol Explanation:	Safe water buoy, simplified
S57/INT1	BOYSAW Q 130.5

Symbol Name:	SY(**BOYSPH01**)
Symbol Number:	**55**
Symbol Explanation:	Spherical buoy, paper-chart
S57/INT1	BOYxxx Q 22
	BOYSAW Q 130.5
	BOYSPP Q 130.6

Symbol Name:	SY(**BOYSPP11**)
Symbol Number:	**56**
Symbol Explanation:	Special purpose buoy, spherical or barrel shaped, or default symbol for special purpose buoy, simplified
S57/INT1	BOYSPP Q 50-57; 59; 62; 70; 71; 130.6 Q 130.6

Symbol Name:	SY(**BOYSPP15**)
Symbol Number:	**57**
Symbol Explanation:	Special purpose TSS buoy marking the starboard side of the traffic lane, simplified
S57/INT1	BOYSPP Q 130.6

Symbol Name:	SY(**BOYSPP25**)
Symbol Number:	**58**
Symbol Explanation:	Special purpose TSS buoy marking the port side of the traffic lane, simplified
S57/INT1	BOYSPP Q 130.6

Symbol Name:	SY(**BOYSPR01**)
Symbol Number:	**59**
Symbol Explanation:	Spar buoy, paper-chart
S57/INT1	BOYxxx Q 24
	BOYCAR Q 130.3
	BOYISD Q 130.4
	BOYLAT Q 130.1
	BOYSAW Q 130.5
	BOYSPP Q 130.6

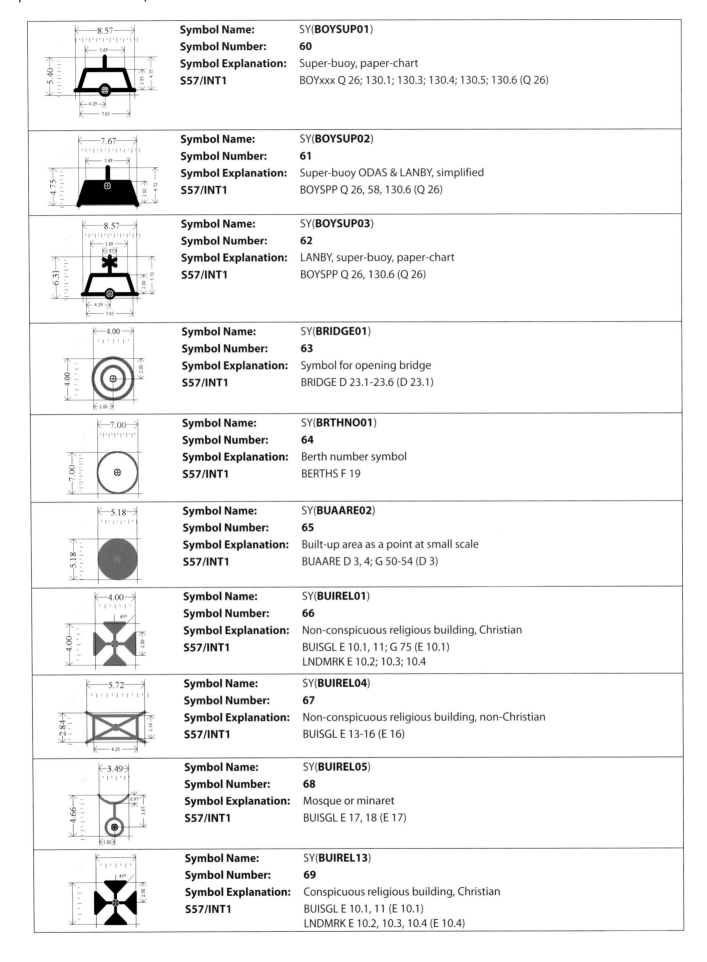

	Symbol Name:	SY(**BOYSUP01**)
	Symbol Number:	**60**
	Symbol Explanation:	Super-buoy, paper-chart
	S57/INT1	BOYxxx Q 26; 130.1; 130.3; 130.4; 130.5; 130.6 (Q 26)

	Symbol Name:	SY(**BOYSUP02**)
	Symbol Number:	**61**
	Symbol Explanation:	Super-buoy ODAS & LANBY, simplified
	S57/INT1	BOYSPP Q 26, 58, 130.6 (Q 26)

	Symbol Name:	SY(**BOYSUP03**)
	Symbol Number:	**62**
	Symbol Explanation:	LANBY, super-buoy, paper-chart
	S57/INT1	BOYSPP Q 26, 130.6 (Q 26)

	Symbol Name:	SY(**BRIDGE01**)
	Symbol Number:	**63**
	Symbol Explanation:	Symbol for opening bridge
	S57/INT1	BRIDGE D 23.1-23.6 (D 23.1)

	Symbol Name:	SY(**BRTHNO01**)
	Symbol Number:	**64**
	Symbol Explanation:	Berth number symbol
	S57/INT1	BERTHS F 19

	Symbol Name:	SY(**BUAARE02**)
	Symbol Number:	**65**
	Symbol Explanation:	Built-up area as a point at small scale
	S57/INT1	BUAARE D 3, 4; G 50-54 (D 3)

	Symbol Name:	SY(**BUIREL01**)
	Symbol Number:	**66**
	Symbol Explanation:	Non-conspicuous religious building, Christian
	S57/INT1	BUISGL E 10.1, 11; G 75 (E 10.1)
		LNDMRK E 10.2; 10.3; 10.4

	Symbol Name:	SY(**BUIREL04**)
	Symbol Number:	**67**
	Symbol Explanation:	Non-conspicuous religious building, non-Christian
	S57/INT1	BUISGL E 13-16 (E 16)

	Symbol Name:	SY(**BUIREL05**)
	Symbol Number:	**68**
	Symbol Explanation:	Mosque or minaret
	S57/INT1	BUISGL E 17, 18 (E 17)

	Symbol Name:	SY(**BUIREL13**)
	Symbol Number:	**69**
	Symbol Explanation:	Conspicuous religious building, Christian
	S57/INT1	BUISGL E 10.1, 11 (E 10.1)
		LNDMRK E 10.2, 10.3, 10.4 (E 10.4)

	Symbol Name:	SY(**BUIREL14**)
	Symbol Number:	**70**
	Symbol Explanation:	Conspicuous religious building, non-Christian
	S57/INT1	BUISGL E 13-16 (E 16)

	Symbol Name:	SY(**BUIREL15**)
	Symbol Number:	**71**
	Symbol Explanation:	Conspicuous mosque or minaret
	S57/INT1	BUISGL E 17, 18 (E 17)

	Symbol Name:	SY(**BUISGL01**)
	Symbol Number:	**72**
	Symbol Explanation:	Single building
	S57/INT1	BUISGL D 5, 6, 8; G 60-63, 71, 76, 83, 84, 93, 95, 97 (D 5)

	Symbol Name:	SY(**BUISGL11**)
	Symbol Number:	**73**
	Symbol Explanation:	Conspicuous single building
	S57/INT1	BUISGL D 5, 6, 8; G 60-63, 71, 76, 83, 84, 93, 95, 97 (D 5)

	Symbol Name:	SY(**CAIRNS01**)
	Symbol Number:	**74**
	Symbol Explanation:	Cairn
	S57/INT1	BCNSPP Q 100
		LNDMRK Q 100 (Q 100)

	Symbol Name:	SY(**CAIRNS11**)
	Symbol Number:	**75**
	Symbol Explanation:	Conspicuous cairn
	S57/INT1	BCNSPP Q 100
		LNDMRK Q 100 (Q 100)

	Symbol Name:	SY(**CBLARE51**)
	Symbol Number:	**76**
	Symbol Explanation:	Cable area
	S57/INT1	CBLARE L 30.2, 31.2 (L 31.2)

	Symbol Name:	SY(**CGUSTA02**)
	Symbol Number:	**77**
	Symbol Explanation:	Coastguard station
	S57/INT1	CGUSTA T 10, 11

	Symbol Name:	SY(**CHCRDEL1**)
	Symbol Number:	**78**
	Symbol Explanation:	This object has been manually deleted or modified
	S57/INT1	N/A

	Symbol Name:	SY(**CHCRID01**)
	Symbol Number:	**79**
	Symbol Explanation:	This object has been manually updated
	S57/INT1	N/A

	Symbol Name: SY(**CHIMNY01**) **Symbol Number:** 80 **Symbol Explanation:** Chimney **S57/INT1** LNDMRK E 22
	Symbol Name: SY(**CHIMNY11**) **Symbol Number:** 81 **Symbol Explanation:** Conspicuous chimney **S57/INT1** LNDMRK E 22
	Symbol Name: SY(**CHINFO06**) **Symbol Number:** 82 **Symbol Explanation:** HO caution note **S57/INT1** CTNARE M 29.2 DAMCON F 44 MIPARE N 30-33 (N 30) SPLARE N 13
	Symbol Name: SY(**CHINFO07**) **Symbol Number:** 83 **Symbol Explanation:** HO information note **S57/INT1** CTSARE N 64 DMPGRD N 23, 24, 62.1, 62.2 (N 62.2) HRBFAC F 10, 50, 52; U 1.1 (U 1.1) ICNARE N 65 M_NPUB Not specified PIPARE L 40.2, 41.2 (L 40.1)
	Symbol Name: SY(**CHINFO08**) **Symbol Number:** 84 **Symbol Explanation:** Mariner's information note **S57/INT1** **marnot** - to meet the requirement of IMO PS 1.6
	Symbol Name: SY(**CHINFO09**) **Symbol Number:** 85 **Symbol Explanation:** Mariners caution note **S57/INT1** **marfea** - to meet the requirement of IMO PS 1.6 and of IHO S-52 sections 1.1 and 5.5 **marnot** - to meet the requirement of IMO PS 1.6
	Symbol Name: SY(**CHINFO10**) **Symbol Number:** 86 **Symbol Explanation:** Manufacturer's information note **S57/INT1** **mnufea** - to implement IMO PS section 2 and IHO S-52 section 2
	Symbol Name: SY(**CHINFO11**) **Symbol Number:** 87 **Symbol Explanation:** Manufacturer's caution note **S57/INT1** **mnufea** - to implement IMO PS section 2 and IHO S-52 section 2
	Symbol Name: SY(**CHKSYM01**) **Symbol Number:** 88 **Symbol Explanation:** Test symbol for checking symbol sizes, should measure 5 mm by 5 mm **S57/INT1** N/A

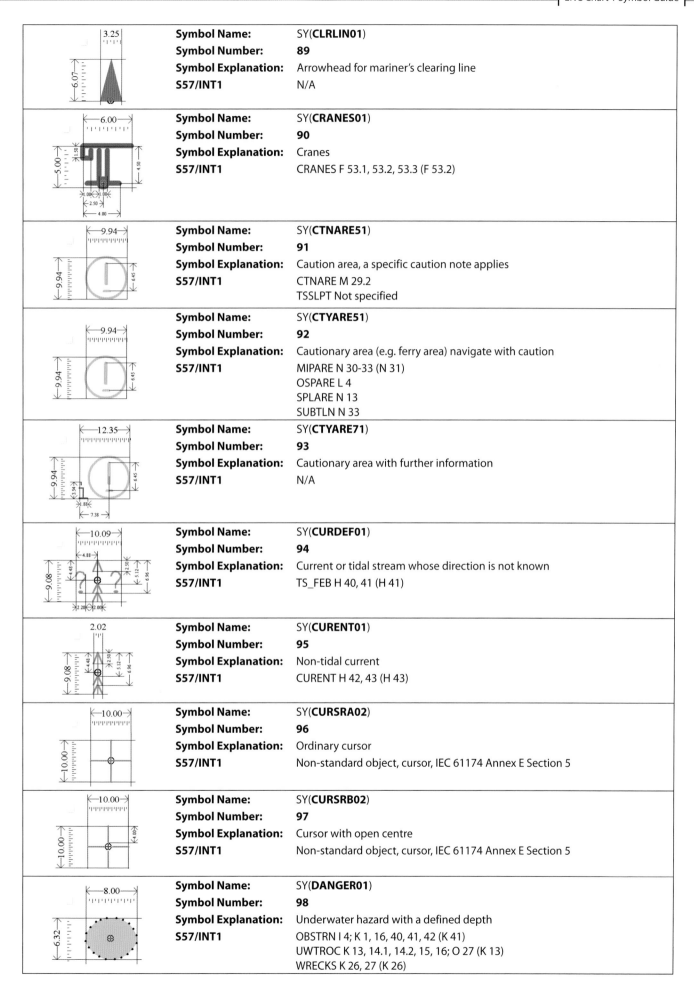

	Symbol Name:	SY(**CLRLIN01**)
	Symbol Number:	**89**
	Symbol Explanation:	Arrowhead for mariner's clearing line
	S57/INT1	N/A

	Symbol Name:	SY(**CRANES01**)
	Symbol Number:	**90**
	Symbol Explanation:	Cranes
	S57/INT1	CRANES F 53.1, 53.2, 53.3 (F 53.2)

	Symbol Name:	SY(**CTNARE51**)
	Symbol Number:	**91**
	Symbol Explanation:	Caution area, a specific caution note applies
	S57/INT1	CTNARE M 29.2
		TSSLPT Not specified

	Symbol Name:	SY(**CTYARE51**)
	Symbol Number:	**92**
	Symbol Explanation:	Cautionary area (e.g. ferry area) navigate with caution
	S57/INT1	MIPARE N 30-33 (N 31)
		OSPARE L 4
		SPLARE N 13
		SUBTLN N 33

	Symbol Name:	SY(**CTYARE71**)
	Symbol Number:	**93**
	Symbol Explanation:	Cautionary area with further information
	S57/INT1	N/A

	Symbol Name:	SY(**CURDEF01**)
	Symbol Number:	**94**
	Symbol Explanation:	Current or tidal stream whose direction is not known
	S57/INT1	TS_FEB H 40, 41 (H 41)

	Symbol Name:	SY(**CURENT01**)
	Symbol Number:	**95**
	Symbol Explanation:	Non-tidal current
	S57/INT1	CURENT H 42, 43 (H 43)

	Symbol Name:	SY(**CURSRA02**)
	Symbol Number:	**96**
	Symbol Explanation:	Ordinary cursor
	S57/INT1	Non-standard object, cursor, IEC 61174 Annex E Section 5

	Symbol Name:	SY(**CURSRB02**)
	Symbol Number:	**97**
	Symbol Explanation:	Cursor with open centre
	S57/INT1	Non-standard object, cursor, IEC 61174 Annex E Section 5

	Symbol Name:	SY(**DANGER01**)
	Symbol Number:	**98**
	Symbol Explanation:	Underwater hazard with a defined depth
	S57/INT1	OBSTRN I 4; K 1, 16, 40, 41, 42 (K 41)
		UWTROC K 13, 14.1, 14.2, 15, 16; O 27 (K 13)
		WRECKS K 26, 27 (K 26)

	Symbol Name:	SY(**DANGER02**)
	Symbol Number:	**99**
	Symbol Explanation:	Underwater hazard with depth greater than 20 metres
	S57/INT1	OBSTRN I 2, 4; K 41, 42, 46.2; L 20, 21.2, 43; Q 42 (K 41) UWTROC K 11, 14.1, 14.2, 15; O 27 (K 14.2) WRECKS K 26, 27, 30 (K 27)
	Symbol Name:	SY(**DAYSQR01**)
	Symbol Number:	**100**
	Symbol Explanation:	Square or rectangular day mark, simplified
	S57/INT1	DAYMAR Q 101
	Symbol Name:	SY(**DAYSQR21**)
	Symbol Number:	**101**
	Symbol Explanation:	Square or rectangular day mark, paper chart
	S57/INT1	DAYMAR Q 101
	Symbol Name:	SY(**DAYTRI01**)
	Symbol Number:	**102**
	Symbol Explanation:	Triangular day mark, point up, simplified
	S57/INT1	DAYMAR Q 101
	Symbol Name:	SY(**DAYTRI05**)
	Symbol Number:	**103**
	Symbol Explanation:	Triangular day mark, point down, simplified
	S57/INT1	DAYMAR Q 101
	Symbol Name:	SY(**DAYTRI21**)
	Symbol Number:	**104**
	Symbol Explanation:	Triangular day mark, point up, paper chart
	S57/INT1	DAYMAR Q 101
	Symbol Name:	SY(**DAYTRI25**)
	Symbol Number:	**105**
	Symbol Explanation:	Triangular day mark, point down, paper chart
	S57/INT1	DAYMAR Q 101
	Symbol Name:	SY(**DIRBOYA1**)
	Symbol Number:	**106**
	Symbol Explanation:	Direction and colour of buoyage for approaching harbour in IALA region A (red to port)
	S57/INT1	M_NSYS Q 130.1, 130.2 (Q 130.2)
	Symbol Name:	SY(**DIRBOYB1**)
	Symbol Number:	**107**
	Symbol Explanation:	Direction and colour of buoyage for approaching harbour in IALA region B (green to port)
	S57/INT1	M_NSYS Q 130.1, 130.2 (Q 130.2)
	Symbol Name:	SY(**DISMAR03**)
	Symbol Number:	**108**
	Symbol Explanation:	Distance mark
	S57/INT1	DISMAR F 40

	Symbol Name:	SY(**DISMAR04**)
	Symbol Number:	**109**
	Symbol Explanation:	Distance point with no mark
	S57/INT1	DISMAR F 40

	Symbol Name:	SY(**DNGHILIT**)
	Symbol Number:	**110**
	Symbol Explanation:	Transparent danger highlight for mariner's use
	S57/INT1	Non-standard object **dnghlt** IEC 61174 Annex E Section 14

	Symbol Name:	SY(**DOMES001**)
	Symbol Number:	**111**
	Symbol Explanation:	Dome
	S57/INT1	LNDMRK E 10.4, 30.4 (E 10.4) (E 30.4)

	Symbol Name:	SY(**DOMES011**)
	Symbol Number:	**112**
	Symbol Explanation:	Conspicuous dome
	S57/INT1	LNDMRK E 2, 10.4, 30.4 (E 10.4) (E 30.4)

	Symbol Name:	SY(**DSHAER01**)
	Symbol Number:	**113**
	Symbol Explanation:	Dish aerial
	S57/INT1	LNDMRK E 31

	Symbol Name:	SY(**DSHAER11**)
	Symbol Number:	**114**
	Symbol Explanation:	Conspicuous dish aerial
	S57/INT1	LNDMRK E 2, 31

	Symbol Name:	SY(**DWRTPT51**)
	Symbol Number:	**115**
	Symbol Explanation:	Part of deep water route
	S57/INT1	DWRTPT M 27.1-2

	Symbol Name:	SY(**EBBSTR01**)
	Symbol Number:	**116**
	Symbol Explanation:	Ebb stream, rate at spring tides
	S57/INT1	TS_FEB H 40-41 (H 41)

	Symbol Name:	SY(**EBLVRM11**)
	Symbol Number:	**117**
	Symbol Explanation:	Point of origin for an offset EBL or VRM
	S57/INT1	N/A

	Symbol Name:	SY(**ENTRES51**)
	Symbol Number:	**118**
	Symbol Explanation:	Area where entry is prohibited or restricted or to be avoided
	S57/INT1	RESARE M 29.2 N 2.1, 2.2 (N 2.2)

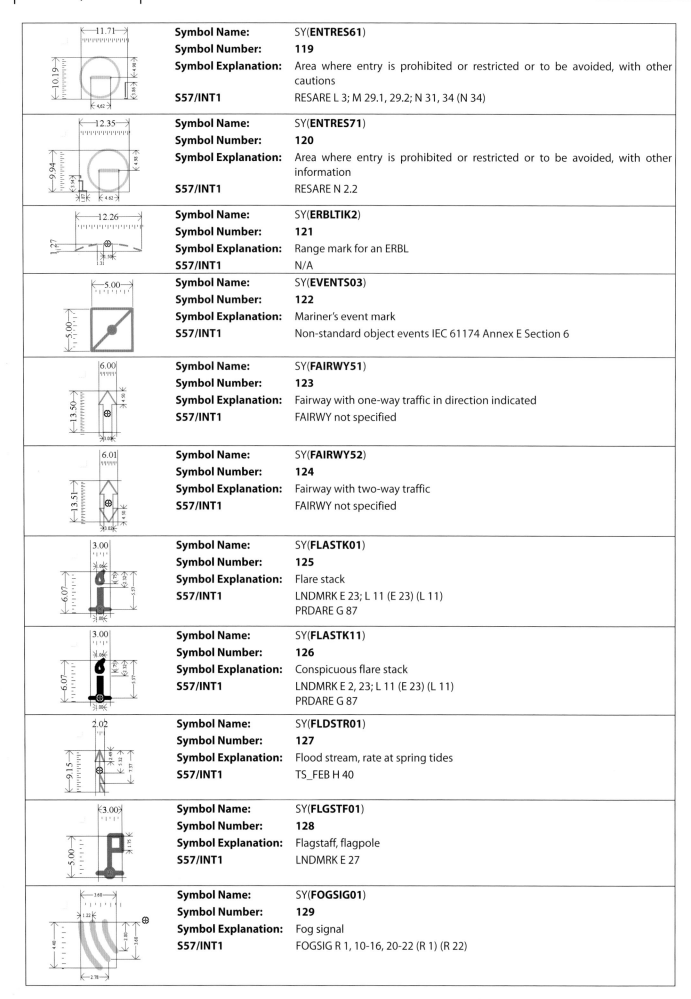

Symbol Name:	SY(**ENTRES61**)
Symbol Number:	**119**
Symbol Explanation:	Area where entry is prohibited or restricted or to be avoided, with other cautions
S57/INT1	RESARE L 3; M 29.1, 29.2; N 31, 34 (N 34)

Symbol Name:	SY(**ENTRES71**)
Symbol Number:	**120**
Symbol Explanation:	Area where entry is prohibited or restricted or to be avoided, with other information
S57/INT1	RESARE N 2.2

Symbol Name:	SY(**ERBLTIK2**)
Symbol Number:	**121**
Symbol Explanation:	Range mark for an ERBL
S57/INT1	N/A

Symbol Name:	SY(**EVENTS03**)
Symbol Number:	**122**
Symbol Explanation:	Mariner's event mark
S57/INT1	Non-standard object events IEC 61174 Annex E Section 6

Symbol Name:	SY(**FAIRWY51**)
Symbol Number:	**123**
Symbol Explanation:	Fairway with one-way traffic in direction indicated
S57/INT1	FAIRWY not specified

Symbol Name:	SY(**FAIRWY52**)
Symbol Number:	**124**
Symbol Explanation:	Fairway with two-way traffic
S57/INT1	FAIRWY not specified

Symbol Name:	SY(**FLASTK01**)
Symbol Number:	**125**
Symbol Explanation:	Flare stack
S57/INT1	LNDMRK E 23; L 11 (E 23) (L 11) PRDARE G 87

Symbol Name:	SY(**FLASTK11**)
Symbol Number:	**126**
Symbol Explanation:	Conspicuous flare stack
S57/INT1	LNDMRK E 2, 23; L 11 (E 23) (L 11) PRDARE G 87

Symbol Name:	SY(**FLDSTR01**)
Symbol Number:	**127**
Symbol Explanation:	Flood stream, rate at spring tides
S57/INT1	TS_FEB H 40

Symbol Name:	SY(**FLGSTF01**)
Symbol Number:	**128**
Symbol Explanation:	Flagstaff, flagpole
S57/INT1	LNDMRK E 27

Symbol Name:	SY(**FOGSIG01**)
Symbol Number:	**129**
Symbol Explanation:	Fog signal
S57/INT1	FOGSIG R 1, 10-16, 20-22 (R 1) (R 22)

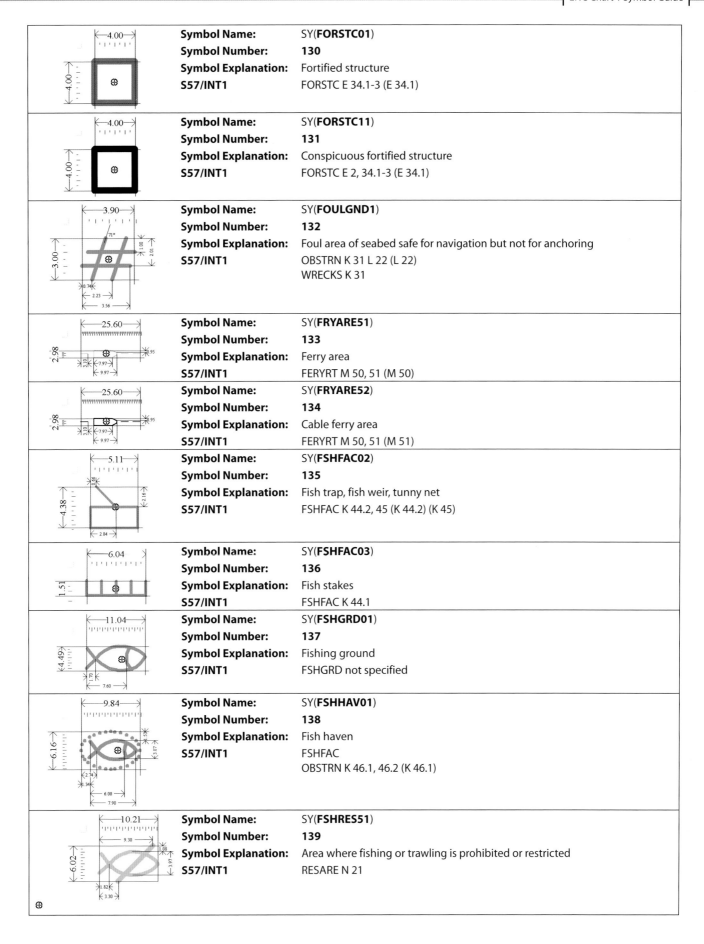

Symbol Name:	SY(**FORSTC01**)	
Symbol Number:	**130**	
Symbol Explanation:	Fortified structure	
S57/INT1	FORSTC E 34.1-3 (E 34.1)	
Symbol Name:	SY(**FORSTC11**)	
Symbol Number:	**131**	
Symbol Explanation:	Conspicuous fortified structure	
S57/INT1	FORSTC E 2, 34.1-3 (E 34.1)	
Symbol Name:	SY(**FOULGND1**)	
Symbol Number:	**132**	
Symbol Explanation:	Foul area of seabed safe for navigation but not for anchoring	
S57/INT1	OBSTRN K 31 L 22 (L 22) WRECKS K 31	
Symbol Name:	SY(**FRYARE51**)	
Symbol Number:	**133**	
Symbol Explanation:	Ferry area	
S57/INT1	FERYRT M 50, 51 (M 50)	
Symbol Name:	SY(**FRYARE52**)	
Symbol Number:	**134**	
Symbol Explanation:	Cable ferry area	
S57/INT1	FERYRT M 50, 51 (M 51)	
Symbol Name:	SY(**FSHFAC02**)	
Symbol Number:	**135**	
Symbol Explanation:	Fish trap, fish weir, tunny net	
S57/INT1	FSHFAC K 44.2, 45 (K 44.2) (K 45)	
Symbol Name:	SY(**FSHFAC03**)	
Symbol Number:	**136**	
Symbol Explanation:	Fish stakes	
S57/INT1	FSHFAC K 44.1	
Symbol Name:	SY(**FSHGRD01**)	
Symbol Number:	**137**	
Symbol Explanation:	Fishing ground	
S57/INT1	FSHGRD not specified	
Symbol Name:	SY(**FSHHAV01**)	
Symbol Number:	**138**	
Symbol Explanation:	Fish haven	
S57/INT1	FSHFAC OBSTRN K 46.1, 46.2 (K 46.1)	
Symbol Name:	SY(**FSHRES51**)	
Symbol Number:	**139**	
Symbol Explanation:	Area where fishing or trawling is prohibited or restricted	
S57/INT1	RESARE N 21	

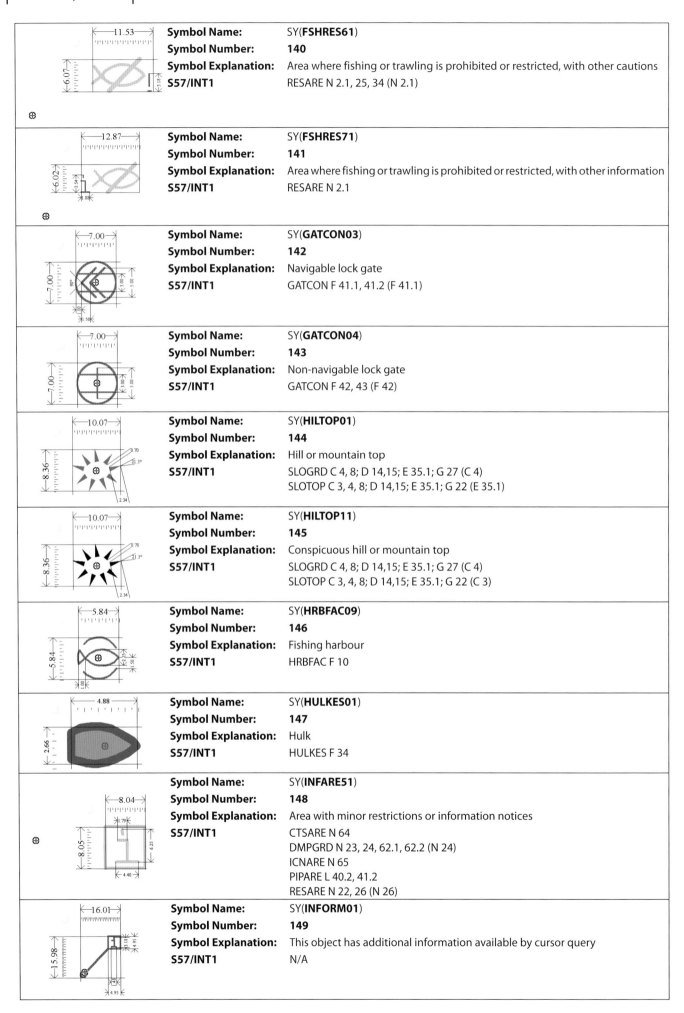

	Symbol Name:	SY(**FSHRES61**)
	Symbol Number:	**140**
	Symbol Explanation:	Area where fishing or trawling is prohibited or restricted, with other cautions
	S57/INT1	RESARE N 2.1, 25, 34 (N 2.1)

	Symbol Name:	SY(**FSHRES71**)
	Symbol Number:	**141**
	Symbol Explanation:	Area where fishing or trawling is prohibited or restricted, with other information
	S57/INT1	RESARE N 2.1

	Symbol Name:	SY(**GATCON03**)
	Symbol Number:	**142**
	Symbol Explanation:	Navigable lock gate
	S57/INT1	GATCON F 41.1, 41.2 (F 41.1)

	Symbol Name:	SY(**GATCON04**)
	Symbol Number:	**143**
	Symbol Explanation:	Non-navigable lock gate
	S57/INT1	GATCON F 42, 43 (F 42)

	Symbol Name:	SY(**HILTOP01**)
	Symbol Number:	**144**
	Symbol Explanation:	Hill or mountain top
	S57/INT1	SLOGRD C 4, 8; D 14,15; E 35.1; G 27 (C 4)
		SLOTOP C 3, 4, 8; D 14,15; E 35.1; G 22 (E 35.1)

	Symbol Name:	SY(**HILTOP11**)
	Symbol Number:	**145**
	Symbol Explanation:	Conspicuous hill or mountain top
	S57/INT1	SLOGRD C 4, 8; D 14,15; E 35.1; G 27 (C 4)
		SLOTOP C 3, 4, 8; D 14,15; E 35.1; G 22 (C 3)

	Symbol Name:	SY(**HRBFAC09**)
	Symbol Number:	**146**
	Symbol Explanation:	Fishing harbour
	S57/INT1	HRBFAC F 10

	Symbol Name:	SY(**HULKES01**)
	Symbol Number:	**147**
	Symbol Explanation:	Hulk
	S57/INT1	HULKES F 34

	Symbol Name:	SY(**INFARE51**)
	Symbol Number:	**148**
	Symbol Explanation:	Area with minor restrictions or information notices
	S57/INT1	CTSARE N 64
		DMPGRD N 23, 24, 62.1, 62.2 (N 24)
		ICNARE N 65
		PIPARE L 40.2, 41.2
		RESARE N 22, 26 (N 26)

	Symbol Name:	SY(**INFORM01**)
	Symbol Number:	**149**
	Symbol Explanation:	This object has additional information available by cursor query
	S57/INT1	N/A

	Symbol Name:	SY(**ISODGR01**)
	Symbol Number:	**150**
	Symbol Explanation:	Isolated danger of depth less than the safety contour
	S57/INT1	OBSTRN I 2, 4; K 1, 31, 40-43.2, 46.1, 46.2; L 20, 21.1-21.3, 22, 43 (I 2)
		UWTROC K 11, 13-14.2, 16; O 27 (K 11)
		WRECKS K 26-31 (K 26)
	Symbol Name:	SY(**ITZARE51**)
	Symbol Number:	**151**
	Symbol Explanation:	Area of inshore traffic
	S57/INT1	ISTZNE M 14, 25.1, 25.2 (M 14)
	Symbol Name:	SY(**LIGHTS11**)
	Symbol Number:	**152**
	Symbol Explanation:	Light flare, red
	S57/INT1	LIGHTS G 117; P 1-6, 10.1-11, 11.2, 12-14, 16, 20.1, 30.1-30.3, 31, 40, 41, 43, 45-62, 65; Q 41; R 20, 22 (P 46)
	Symbol Name:	SY(**LIGHTS12**)
	Symbol Number:	**153**
	Symbol Explanation:	Light flare, green
	S57/INT1	LIGHTS G 117; P 1-11, 11.3, 12-62, 65; Q 41; R 20, 22 (P 21)
	Symbol Name:	SY(**LIGHTS13**)
	Symbol Number:	**154**
	Symbol Explanation:	Light flare, white or yellow
	S57/INT1	LIGHTS G 117; P 1-11, 11.1, 11.6, 11.7, 11.8, 12-62, 65; Q 41, 130.3; R 20, 22 (Q 41)
	Symbol Name:	SY(**LIGHTS81**)
	Symbol Number:	**155**
	Symbol Explanation:	Strip light
	S57/INT1	LIGHTS P 64
	Symbol Name:	SY(**LIGHTS82**)
	Symbol Number:	**156**
	Symbol Explanation:	Floodlight
	S57/INT1	LIGHTS G 70; P 63 (P 63)
	Symbol Name:	SY(**LITDEF11**)
	Symbol Number:	**157**
	Symbol Explanation:	Light flare
	S57/INT1	LIGHTS G 117; P 1-10, 11, 12-15, 20.1-20.3, 22-61.1, 62; Q 41; R 20, 22 (P 2)
	Symbol Name:	SY(**LITFLT01**)
	Symbol Number:	**158**
	Symbol Explanation:	Light float, paper-chart
	S57/INT1	LITFLT Q 30-31 (Q 30) (Q 31)
	Symbol Name:	SY(**LITFLT02**)
	Symbol Number:	**159**
	Symbol Explanation:	Light float, simplified
	S57/INT1	LITFLT Q 30-31 (Q 30) (Q 31)

	Symbol Name:	SY(**LITVES01**)
	Symbol Number:	**160**
	Symbol Explanation:	Light vessel, paper-chart
	S57/INT1	LITVES P 6

	Symbol Name:	SY(**LITVES02**)
	Symbol Number:	**161**
	Symbol Explanation:	Light vessel, simplified
	S57/INT1	LITVES P 6

	Symbol Name:	SY(**LNDARE01**)
	Symbol Number:	**162**
	Symbol Explanation:	Land as a point at small scale
	S57/INT1	LNDARE K 10

	Symbol Name:	SY(**LOCMAG01**)
	Symbol Number:	**163**
	Symbol Explanation:	Cursor pick site for a magnetic anomaly at a point or along a line
	S57/INT1	LOCMAG B 82.1-2 (B 82.1)

	Symbol Name:	SY(**LOCMAG51**)
	Symbol Number:	**164**
	Symbol Explanation:	Cursor pick site for a magnetic anomaly over an area
	S57/INT1	LOCMAG B 82.1-2 (B 82.2)

	Symbol Name:	SY(**LOWACC01**)
	Symbol Number:	**165**
	Symbol Explanation:	Point feature or area of low accuracy
	S57/INT1	Not specified B 7, 8; I 3.1, 3.2 (B 7)
		COALNE C 2, 12, 32, 33
		DEPCNT I 31
		OBSTRN K 43.2
		SOUNDG I 4, 14not specified B 7, 8; I 3.1, 3.2 (B 7)
		COALNE C 2, 12, 32, 33
		DEPCNT I 31
		OBSTRN K 43.2
		SOUNDG I 4, 14

	Symbol Name:	SY(**MAGVAR01**)
	Symbol Number:	**166**
	Symbol Explanation:	Cursor pick site for magnetic variation at a point
	S57/INT1	MAGVAR B 60, 66, 68.1, 70, 71

	Symbol Name:	SY(**MAGVAR51**)
	Symbol Number:	**167**
	Symbol Explanation:	Cursor pick site for magnetic variation along a line or over an area
	S57/INT1	MAGVAR B 60, 66, 70, 71

	Symbol Name:	SY(**MARCUL02**)
	Symbol Number:	**168**
	Symbol Explanation:	Fish farm
	S57/INT1	MARCUL K 47, 48.1 – 2 (K 48.1)

Symbol Name:	SY(**MONUMT02**)
Symbol Number:	**169**
Symbol Explanation:	Monument
S57/INT1	LNDMRK E 24; G 66 (E 24)

Symbol Name:	SY(**MONUMT12**)
Symbol Number:	**170**
Symbol Explanation:	Conspicuous monument
S57/INT1	LNDMRK E 2, 24; G 66 (E 24)

Symbol Name:	SY(**MORFAC03**)
Symbol Number:	**171**
Symbol Explanation:	Mooring dolphin
S57/INT1	MORFAC F 20 SLCONS G 171

Symbol Name:	SY(**MORFAC04**)
Symbol Number:	**172**
Symbol Explanation:	Deviation mooring dolphin
S57/INT1	MORFAC F 21

Symbol Name:	SY(**MSTCON04**)
Symbol Number:	**173**
Symbol Explanation:	Mast
S57/INT1	LNDMRK E 28, 30.1; G 67, 69; P 61.1, 61.2 (E 28)

Symbol Name:	SY(**MSTCON14**)
Symbol Number:	**174**
Symbol Explanation:	Conspicuous mast
S57/INT1	LNDMRK E 28, 30.1; G 67, 69; P 61.1, 61.2 (E 30.1)

Symbol Name:	SY(**NORTHAR1**)
Symbol Number:	**175**
Symbol Explanation:	North arrow
S57/INT1	N/A

Symbol Name:	SY(**NOTBRD11**)
Symbol Number:	**176**
Symbol Explanation:	Conspicuous notice board
S57/INT1	BCNSPP Q 126

Symbol Name:	SY(**OBSTRN01**)
Symbol Number:	**177**
Symbol Explanation:	Obstruction, depth not stated
S57/INT1	OBSTRN I 2, 4; K 1, 16, 40, 42 (K 1)

Symbol Name:	SY(**OBSTRN02**)
Symbol Number:	**178**
Symbol Explanation:	Obstruction in the intertidal area
S57/INT1	N/A

	Symbol Name:	SY(**OBSTRN11**)
	Symbol Number:	**179**
	Symbol Explanation:	Obstruction in the water which is always above water level
	S57/INT1	OBSTRN G 179, 180; L 23 (L 23)

	Symbol Name:	SY(**OFSPLF01**)
	Symbol Number:	**180**
	Symbol Explanation:	Offshore platform
	S57/INT1	OFSPLF L 2, 10, 11-15, 17 (L 2)

	Symbol Name:	SY(**OSPONE03**)
	Symbol Number:	**181**
	Symbol Explanation:	One minute mark for own ship vector
	S57/INT1	N/A

	Symbol Name:	SY(**OSPSIX03**)
	Symbol Number:	**182**
	Symbol Explanation:	Six minute mark for own ship vector
	S57/INT1	N/A

	Symbol Name:	SY(**OWNSHP02**)
	Symbol Number:	**183**
	Symbol Explanation:	Own ship symbol, constant size
	S57/INT1	N/A

	Symbol Name:	SY(**OWNSHP05**)
	Symbol Number:	**184**
	Symbol Explanation:	Own ship drawn to scale with conning position marked
	S57/INT1	N/A

	Symbol Name:	SY(**PASTRK03**)
	Symbol Number:	**185**
	Symbol Explanation:	Time mark on past track
	S57/INT1	N/A

	Symbol Name:	SY(**PASTRK04**)
	Symbol Number:	**186**
	Symbol Explanation:	Time mark on secondary past track
	S57/INT1	N/A

	Symbol Name:	SY(**PILBOP02**)
	Symbol Number:	**187**
	Symbol Explanation:	Pilot boarding place
	S57/INT1	PILBOP T 1.1-1.4 (T 1.1)

	Symbol Name:	SY(**PILPNT02**)
	Symbol Number:	**188**
	Symbol Explanation:	Pile or bollard
	S57/INT1	MORFAC G 181 PILPNT F 22; G 179, 180 (F 22)

	Symbol Name:	SY(**PLNPOS01**)
	Symbol Number:	**189**
	Symbol Explanation:	Surrounding ellipse for arrival date and time at planned position
	S57/INT1	Non-standard object **plnpos** IEC 61174 Annex E Section 19

	Symbol Name:	SY(**PLNPOS03**)
	Symbol Number:	**190**
	Symbol Explanation:	Cross line for planned position
	S57/INT1	Non-standard object **plnpos** IEC 61174 Annex E Section 19

Symbol Name:	SY(**PLNSPD03**)	
Symbol Number:	**191**	
Symbol Explanation:	Box for speed to make good, planned route	
S57/INT1	N/A	

Symbol Name:	SY(**PLNSPD04**)	
Symbol Number:	**192**	
Symbol Explanation:	Box for speed to make good, alternate route	
S57/INT1	N/A	

Symbol Name:	SY(**POSGEN01**)	
Symbol Number:	**193**	
Symbol Explanation:	Position of a point feature	
S57/INT1	LNDMRK E 10.3, 17	
	RADSTA M 30; S 1 (M 30)	

Symbol Name:	SY(**POSGEN03**)	
Symbol Number:	**194**	
Symbol Explanation:	Position of a conspicuous point feature	
S57/INT1	BUISGL Not specified	
	LNDMRK E 2, 17	
	PYLONS D 26	

Symbol Name:	SY(**POSGEN04**)	
Symbol Number:	**195**	
Symbol Explanation:	Position of an elevation or control point	
S57/INT1	CHKPNT not specified	
	CTRPNT B 20-24 (B 21)	
	LNDELV C 10-13 G 24, 25; K 10, 20 (C 11)	
	LNDRGN C 33; G 3-12, 20, 21, 23, 26, 29-33, 35, 36	

Symbol Name:	SY(**POSITN03**)	
Symbol Number:	**196**	
Symbol Explanation:	Own ship position fix	
S57/INT1	Non-standard object positn IEC 61174 Annex E Section 7, 8	

Symbol Name:	SY(**PRCARE12**)	
Symbol Number:	**197**	
Symbol Explanation:	Point symbol for traffic precautionary area	
S57/INT1	PRCARE M 16, 24 (M 16)	

Symbol Name:	SY(**PRCARE51**)	
Symbol Number:	**198**	
Symbol Explanation:	Traffic precautionary area	
S57/INT1	PRCARE M 16, 24	

Symbol Name:	SY(**PRDINS02**)	
Symbol Number:	**199**	
Symbol Explanation:	Mine, quarry	
S57/INT1	PRDARE E 35.1, 35.2 (E 35.2)	

Symbol Name:	SY(**PRICKE03**)	
Symbol Number:	**200**	
Symbol Explanation:	Withy, port-hand, paper-chart	
S57/INT1	BCNLAT Q 92	

	Symbol Name:	SY(**PRICKE04**)
	Symbol Number:	**201**
	Symbol Explanation:	Withy, starboard-hand, paper-chart
	S57/INT1	BCNLAT Q 92
	Symbol Name:	SY(**QUAPOS01**)
	Symbol Number:	**202**
	Symbol Explanation:	Position approximate
	S57/INT1	As applicable B 7
	Symbol Name:	SY(**QUARRY01**)
	Symbol Number:	**203**
	Symbol Explanation:	Quarry
	S57/INT1	PRDARE E 35.1, 35.2 (E 35.1)
	Symbol Name:	SY(**QUESMRK1**)
	Symbol Number:	**204**
	Symbol Explanation:	Object which is not sufficiently described to be symbolized, or for which no symbol exists in the symbol library
	S57/INT1	Not specified
	Symbol Name:	SY(**RACNSP01**)
	Symbol Number:	**205**
	Symbol Explanation:	Symbol indicating this object is radar conspicuous
	S57/INT1	Not specified S 4, 5 (S 5) CBLOHD D 26 CONVYR D 25; G 182 PIPOHD D 28
	Symbol Name:	SY(**RADRFL03**)
	Symbol Number:	**206**
	Symbol Explanation:	Radar reflector
	S57/INT1	RADRFL Not specified
	Symbol Name:	SY(**RASCAN01**)
	Symbol Number:	**207**
	Symbol Explanation:	Radar scanner
	S57/INT1	LNDMRK E 30.3
	Symbol Name:	SY(**RASCAN11**)
	Symbol Number:	**208**
	Symbol Explanation:	Conspicuous radar scanner
	S57/INT1	LNDMRK E 2, 30.3 (E 30.3)
	Symbol Name:	SY(**RCLDEF01**)
	Symbol Number:	**209**
	Symbol Explanation:	Radio calling-in point whose direction is not known
	S57/INT1	RDOCAL M 40
	Symbol Name:	SY(**RCTLPT52**)
	Symbol Number:	**210**
	Symbol Explanation:	Recommended traffic direction between parts of a traffic separation scheme, or for ships not needing a deep water route
	S57/INT1	RCTLPT not specified

	Symbol Name:	SY(**RDOCAL02**)
	Symbol Number:	**211**
	Symbol Explanation:	Radio calling-in point for traffic in one direction only
	S57/INT1	RDOCAL M 40
	Symbol Name:	SY(**RDOCAL03**)
	Symbol Number:	**212**
	Symbol Explanation:	Radio calling-in point for traffic in both directions
	S57/INT1	RDOCAL M 40
	Symbol Name:	SY(**RDOSTA02**)
	Symbol Number:	**213**
	Symbol Explanation:	Radio station
	S57/INT1	RADSTA M 30; S 1 (M 30)
		RDOSTA S 10-16 (S 10)
	Symbol Name:	SY(**RECDEF51**)
	Symbol Number:	**214**
	Symbol Explanation:	Recommended track as an area, direction not defined in data
	S57/INT1	RECTRC M 1, 3-4, 5.1, 5.2, 6 (M 6)
	Symbol Name:	SY(**RECTRC55**)
	Symbol Number:	**215**
	Symbol Explanation:	Recommended two-way track as an area, not based on fixed marks
	S57/INT1	RECTRC M 4, 5.2, 6, 32.2 (M 4)
	Symbol Name:	SY(**RECTRC56**)
	Symbol Number:	**216**
	Symbol Explanation:	Recommended two-way track as an area, based on fixed marks
	S57/INT1	RECTRC M 3, 5.2, 6; P 20.1, 20.2, 30.2, (M 3)
	Symbol Name:	SY(**RECTRC57**)
	Symbol Number:	**217**
	Symbol Explanation:	Recommended one-way track as an area, not based on fixed marks
	S57/INT1	RECTRC M 5.1
	Symbol Name:	SY(**RECTRC58**)
	Symbol Number:	**218**
	Symbol Explanation:	Recommended one-way track as an area, based on fixed marks
	S57/INT1	RECTRC M 5.1
	Symbol Name:	SY(**REFPNT02**)
	Symbol Number:	**219**
	Symbol Explanation:	Reference point, 'ghost cursor' (user interface)
	S57/INT1	**refpnt** To meet the requirements of IMO PS 1.6
	Symbol Name:	SY(**RETRFL01**)
	Symbol Number:	**220**
	Symbol Explanation:	Retro reflector, paper chart
	S57/INT1	RETRFL not specified
	Symbol Name:	SY(**RETRFL02**)
	Symbol Number:	**221**
	Symbol Explanation:	Retro reflector, simplified
	S57/INT1	RETRFL not specified

Symbol Name:	SY(**RFNERY01**)
Symbol Number:	**222**
Symbol Explanation:	Refinery
S57/INT1	PRDARE G 87

Symbol Name:	SY(**RFNERY11**)
Symbol Number:	**223**
Symbol Explanation:	Conspicuous refinery
S57/INT1	PRDARE E 2; G 87

Symbol Name:	SY(**ROLROL01**)
Symbol Number:	**224**
Symbol Explanation:	RoRo terminal
S57/INT1	HRBFAC F 50

Symbol Name:	SY(**RSCSTA02**)
Symbol Number:	**225**
Symbol Explanation:	Rescue station
S57/INT1	RSCSTA T 11-14 (T 12)

Symbol Name:	SY(**RSRDEF51**)
Symbol Number:	**226**
Symbol Explanation:	Area in which undefined restrictions exist
S57/INT1	RESARE N 2.1

Symbol Name:	SY(**RTLDEF51**)
Symbol Number:	**227**
Symbol Explanation:	Recommended route between parts of a traffic separation scheme, or for ships not needing a deep water route, with the direction not specified in the data
S57/INT1	RCTLPT not specified

Symbol Name:	SY(**RTPBCN02**)
Symbol Number:	**228**
Symbol Explanation:	Radar transponder beacon
S57/INT1	RTPBCN S 2-3 (S 3)

Symbol Name:	SY(**SCALEB10**)
Symbol Number:	**229**
Symbol Explanation:	One mile scale bar for display scales larger than 1/80,000
S57/INT1	N/A

Symbol Name:	SY(**SCALEB11**)
Symbol Number:	**230**
Symbol Explanation:	10 mile latitude scale for display scales smaller than 1/80,000
S57/INT1	N/A

Symbol Name:	SY(**SILBUI01**)
Symbol Number:	**231**
Symbol Explanation:	Silo
S57/INT1	SILTNK E 33

Symbol Name:	SY(**SILBUI11**)
Symbol Number:	**232**
Symbol Explanation:	Conspicuous silo
S57/INT1	SILTNK E 2, 33 (E 33)

	Symbol Name:	SY(**SISTAT02**)
	Symbol Number:	**233**
	Symbol Explanation:	Signal station
	S57/INT1	SISTAT T 21-25.2, 27 (T 21)
		SISTAW T 20, 26-36 (T 20)

	Symbol Name:	SY(**SMCFAC02**)
	Symbol Number:	**234**
	Symbol Explanation:	Yacht harbour, marina
	S57/INT1	HRBFAC U 1.1, 1.2 (U 1.1)
		SMCFAC F 17; G 93, 131; U 2-13, 15-30

	Symbol Name:	SY(**SNDWAV02**)
	Symbol Number:	**235**
	Symbol Explanation:	Sand waves
	S57/INT1	SNDWAV J 14

	Symbol Name:	SY(**SOUNDG00**)
	Symbol Number:	**236**
	Symbol Explanation:	Deep soundings, greater than safety depth
	S57/INT1	SOUNDG I 2, 4, 10-15; K 17 (I 4)
		OBSTRN I 2, 4; K 41, 42, 46.2; L 20, 21.2; M 43; Q 42 (K 41)
		UWTROC K 11, 12, 14.1, 14.2,15; O 27 (K 14.1)
		WRECKS K 21, 22, 26, 27, 30 (K 26)

	Symbol Name:	SY(**SOUNDG01**)
	Symbol Number:	**237**
	Symbol Explanation:	For deep soundings, greater than safety depth
	S57/INT1	SOUNDG I 2, 4, 10-15; K 17 (I 4)
		OBSTRN I 2, 4; K 41, 42, 46.2; L 20, 21.2; M 43; Q 42 (K 41)
		UWTROC K 11, 12, 14.1, 14.2,15; O 27 (K 14.1)
		WRECKS K 21, 22, 26, 27, 30 (K 26)

	Symbol Name:	SY(**SOUNDG02**)
	Symbol Number:	**238**
	Symbol Explanation:	For deep soundings, greater than safety depth
	S57/INT1	SOUNDG I 2, 4, 10-15; K 17 (I 4)
		OBSTRN I 2, 4; K 41, 42, 46.2; L 20, 21.2; M 43; Q 42 (K 41)
		UWTROC K 11, 12, 14.1, 14.2,15; O 27 (K 14.1)
		WRECKS K 21, 22, 26, 27, 30 (K 26)

	Symbol Name:	SY(**SOUNDG03**)
	Symbol Number:	**239**
	Symbol Explanation:	For deep soundings, greater than safety depth
	S57/INT1	SOUNDG I 2, 4, 10-15; K 17 (I 4)
		OBSTRN I 2, 4; K 41, 42, 46.2; L 20, 21.2; M 43; Q 42 (K 41)
		UWTROC K 11, 12, 14.1, 14.2,15; O 27 (K 14.1)
		WRECKS K 21, 22, 26, 27, 30 (K 26)

	Symbol Name:	SY(**SOUNDG04**)
	Symbol Number:	**240**
	Symbol Explanation:	For deep soundings, greater than safety depth
	S57/INT1	SOUNDG I 2, 4, 10-15; K 17 (I 4)
		OBSTRN I 2, 4; K 41, 42, 46.2; L 20, 21.2; M 43; Q 42 (K 41)
		UWTROC K 11, 12, 14.1, 14.2,15; O 27 (K 14.1)
		WRECKS K 21, 22, 26, 27, 30 (K 26)

	Symbol Name:	SY(**SOUNDG05**)
	Symbol Number:	**241**
	Symbol Explanation:	For deep soundings, greater than safety depth
	S57/INT1	SOUNDG I 2, 4, 10-15; K 17 (I 4)
		OBSTRN I 2, 4; K 41, 42, 46.2; L 20, 21.2; M 43; Q 42 (K 41)
		UWTROC K 11, 12, 14.1, 14.2,15; O 27 (K 14.1)
		WRECKS K 21, 22, 26, 27, 30 (K 26)

	Symbol Name:	SY(**SOUNDG06**)
	Symbol Number:	**242**
	Symbol Explanation:	For deep soundings, greater than safety depth
	S57/INT1	SOUNDG I 2, 4, 10-15; K 17 (I 4)
		OBSTRN I 2, 4; K 41, 42, 46.2; L 20, 21.2; M 43; Q 42 (K 41)
		UWTROC K 11, 12, 14.1, 14.2,15; O 27 (K 14.1)
		WRECKS K 21, 22, 26, 27, 30 (K 26)
	Symbol Name:	SY(**SOUNDG07**)
	Symbol Number:	**243**
	Symbol Explanation:	For deep soundings, greater than safety depth
	S57/INT1	SOUNDG I 2, 4, 10-15; K 17 (I 4)
		OBSTRN I 2, 4; K 41, 42, 46.2; L 20, 21.2; M 43; Q 42 (K 41)
		UWTROC K 11, 12, 14.1, 14.2,15; O 27 (K 14.1)
		WRECKS K 21, 22, 26, 27, 30 (K 26)
	Symbol Name:	SY(**SOUNDG08**)
	Symbol Number:	**244**
	Symbol Explanation:	For deep soundings, greater than safety depth
	S57/INT1	SOUNDG I 2, 4, 10-15; K 17 (I 4)
		OBSTRN I 2, 4; K 41, 42, 46.2; L 20, 21.2; M 43; Q 42 (K 41)
		UWTROC K 11, 12, 14.1, 14.2,15; O 27 (K 14.1)
		WRECKS K 21, 22, 26, 27, 30 (K 26)
	Symbol Name:	SY(**SOUNDG09**)
	Symbol Number:	**245**
	Symbol Explanation:	For deep soundings, greater than safety depth
	S57/INT1	SOUNDG I 2, 4, 10-15; K 17 (I 4)
		OBSTRN I 2, 4; K 41, 42, 46.2; L 20, 21.2; M 43; Q 42 (K 41)
		UWTROC K 11, 12, 14.1, 14.2,15; O 27 (K 14.1)
		WRECKS K 21, 22, 26, 27, 30 (K 26)
	Symbol Name:	SY(**SOUNDG10**)
	Symbol Number:	**246**
	Symbol Explanation:	For deep soundings, greater than safety depth
	S57/INT1	SOUNDG I 2, 4, 10-15; K 17 (I 4)
		OBSTRN I 2, 4; K 41, 42, 46.2; L 20, 21.2; M 43; Q 42 (K 41)
		UWTROC K 11, 12, 14.1, 14.2,15; O 27 (K 14.1)
		WRECKS K 21, 22, 26, 27, 30 (K 26)
	Symbol Name:	SY(**SOUNDG11**)
	Symbol Number:	**247**
	Symbol Explanation:	For deep soundings, greater than safety depth
	S57/INT1	SOUNDG I 2, 4, 10-15; K 17 (I 4)
		OBSTRN I 2, 4; K 41, 42, 46.2; L 20, 21.2; M 43; Q 42 (K 41)
		UWTROC K 11, 12, 14.1, 14.2,15; O 27 (K 14.1)
		WRECKS K 21, 22, 26, 27, 30 (K 26)
	Symbol Name:	SY(**SOUNDG12**)
	Symbol Number:	**248**
	Symbol Explanation:	For deep soundings, greater than safety depth
	S57/INT1	SOUNDG I 2, 4, 10-15; K 17 (I 4)
		OBSTRN I 2, 4; K 41, 42, 46.2; L 20, 21.2; M 43; Q 42 (K 41)
		UWTROC K 11, 12, 14.1, 14.2,15; O 27 (K 14.1)
		WRECKS K 21, 22, 26, 27, 30 (K 26)
	Symbol Name:	SY(**SOUNDG13**)
	Symbol Number:	**249**
	Symbol Explanation:	For deep soundings, greater than safety depth
	S57/INT1	SOUNDG I 2, 4, 10-15; K 17 (I 4)
		OBSTRN I 2, 4; K 41, 42, 46.2; L 20, 21.2; M 43; Q 42 (K 41)
		UWTROC K 11, 12, 14.1, 14.2,15; O 27 (K 14.1)
		WRECKS K 21, 22, 26, 27, 30 (K 26)

	Symbol Name:	SY(**SOUNDG14**)
	Symbol Number:	**250**
	Symbol Explanation:	For deep soundings, greater than safety depth
	S57/INT1	SOUNDG I 2, 4, 10-15; K 17 (I 4)
		OBSTRN I 2, 4; K 41, 42, 46.2; L 20, 21.2; M 43; Q 42 (K 41)
		UWTROC K 11, 12, 14.1, 14.2,15; O 27 (K 14.1)
		WRECKS K 21, 22, 26, 27, 30 (K 26)
	Symbol Name:	SY(**SOUNDG15**)
	Symbol Number:	**251**
	Symbol Explanation:	For deep soundings, greater than safety depth
	S57/INT1	SOUNDG I 2, 4, 10-15; K 17 (I 4)
		OBSTRN I 2, 4; K 41, 42, 46.2; L 20, 21.2; M 43; Q 42 (K 41)
		UWTROC K 11, 12, 14.1, 14.2,15; O 27 (K 14.1)
		WRECKS K 21, 22, 26, 27, 30 (K 26)
	Symbol Name:	SY(**SOUNDG16**)
	Symbol Number:	**252**
	Symbol Explanation:	For deep soundings, greater than safety depth
	S57/INT1	SOUNDG I 2, 4, 10-15; K 17 (I 4)
		OBSTRN I 2, 4; K 41, 42, 46.2; L 20, 21.2; M 43; Q 42 (K 41)
		UWTROC K 11, 12, 14.1, 14.2,15; O 27 (K 14.1)
		WRECKS K 21, 22, 26, 27, 30 (K 26)
	Symbol Name:	SY(**SOUNDG17**)
	Symbol Number:	**253**
	Symbol Explanation:	For deep soundings, greater than safety depth
	S57/INT1	SOUNDG I 2, 4, 10-15; K 17 (I 4)
		OBSTRN I 2, 4; K 41, 42, 46.2; L 20, 21.2; M 43; Q 42 (K 41)
		UWTROC K 11, 12, 14.1, 14.2,15; O 27 (K 14.1)
		WRECKS K 21, 22, 26, 27, 30 (K 26)
	Symbol Name:	SY(**SOUNDG18**)
	Symbol Number:	**254**
	Symbol Explanation:	For deep soundings, greater than safety depth
	S57/INT1	SOUNDG I 2, 4, 10-15; K 17 (I 4)
		OBSTRN I 2, 4; K 41, 42, 46.2; L 20, 21.2; M 43; Q 42 (K 41)
		UWTROC K 11, 12, 14.1, 14.2,15; O 27 (K 14.1)
		WRECKS K 21, 22, 26, 27, 30 (K 26)
	Symbol Name:	SY(**SOUNDG19**)
	Symbol Number:	**255**
	Symbol Explanation:	For deep soundings, greater than safety depth
	S57/INT1	SOUNDG I 2, 4, 10-15; K 17 (I 4)
		OBSTRN I 2, 4; K 41, 42, 46.2; L 20, 21.2; M 43; Q 42 (K 41)
		UWTROC K 11, 12, 14.1, 14.2,15; O 27 (K 14.1)
		WRECKS K 21, 22, 26, 27, 30 (K 26)
	Symbol Name:	SY(**SOUNDG20**)
	Symbol Number:	**256**
	Symbol Explanation:	For deep soundings, greater than safety depth
	S57/INT1	SOUNDG I 2, 4, 10-15; K 17 (I 4)
		OBSTRN I 2, 4; K 41, 42, 46.2; L 20, 21.2; M 43; Q 42 (K 41)
		UWTROC K 11, 12, 14.1, 14.2,15; O 27 (K 14.1)
		WRECKS K 21, 22, 26, 27, 30 (K 26)
	Symbol Name:	SY(**SOUNDG21**)
	Symbol Number:	**257**
	Symbol Explanation:	For deep soundings, greater than safety depth
	S57/INT1	SOUNDG I 2, 4, 10-15; K 17 (I 4)
		OBSTRN I 2, 4; K 41, 42, 46.2; L 20, 21.2; M 43; Q 42 (K 41)
		UWTROC K 11, 12, 14.1, 14.2,15; O 27 (K 14.1)
		WRECKS K 21, 22, 26, 27, 30 (K 26)

	Symbol Name:	SY(**SOUNDG22**)
	Symbol Number:	**258**
	Symbol Explanation:	For deep soundings, greater than safety depth
	S57/INT1	SOUNDG I 2, 4, 10-15; K 17 (I 4)
		OBSTRN I 2, 4; K 41, 42, 46.2; L 20, 21.2; M 43; Q 42 (K 41)
		UWTROC K 11, 12, 14.1, 14.2,15; O 27 (K 14.1)
		WRECKS K 21, 22, 26, 27, 30 (K 26)
	Symbol Name:	SY(**SOUNDG23**)
	Symbol Number:	**259**
	Symbol Explanation:	For deep soundings, greater than safety depth
	S57/INT1	SOUNDG I 2, 4, 10-15; K 17 (I 4)
		OBSTRN I 2, 4; K 41, 42, 46.2; L 20, 21.2; M 43; Q 42 (K 41)
		UWTROC K 11, 12, 14.1, 14.2,15; O 27 (K 14.1)
		WRECKS K 21, 22, 26, 27, 30 (K 26)
	Symbol Name:	SY(**SOUNDG24**)
	Symbol Number:	**260**
	Symbol Explanation:	For deep soundings, greater than safety depth
	S57/INT1	SOUNDG I 2, 4, 10-15; K 17 (I 4)
		OBSTRN I 2, 4; K 41, 42, 46.2; L 20, 21.2; M 43; Q 42 (K 41)
		UWTROC K 11, 12, 14.1, 14.2,15; O 27 (K 14.1)
		WRECKS K 21, 22, 26, 27, 30 (K 26)
	Symbol Name:	SY(**SOUNDG25**)
	Symbol Number:	**261**
	Symbol Explanation:	For deep soundings, greater than safety depth
	S57/INT1	SOUNDG I 2, 4, 10-15; K 17 (I 4)
		OBSTRN I 2, 4; K 41, 42, 46.2; L 20, 21.2; M 43; Q 42 (K 41)
		UWTROC K 11, 12, 14.1, 14.2,15; O 27 (K 14.1)
		WRECKS K 21, 22, 26, 27, 30 (K 26)
	Symbol Name:	SY(**SOUNDG26**)
	Symbol Number:	**262**
	Symbol Explanation:	For deep soundings, greater than safety depth
	S57/INT1	SOUNDG I 2, 4, 10-15; K 17 (I 4)
		OBSTRN I 2, 4; K 41, 42, 46.2; L 20, 21.2; M 43; Q 42 (K 41)
		UWTROC K 11, 12, 14.1, 14.2,15; O 27 (K 14.1)
		WRECKS K 21, 22, 26, 27, 30 (K 26)
	Symbol Name:	SY(**SOUNDG27**)
	Symbol Number:	**263**
	Symbol Explanation:	For deep soundings, greater than safety depth
	S57/INT1	SOUNDG I 2, 4, 10-15; K 17 (I 4)
		OBSTRN I 2, 4; K 41, 42, 46.2; L 20, 21.2; M 43; Q 42 (K 41)
		UWTROC K 11, 12, 14.1, 14.2,15; O 27 (K 14.1)
		WRECKS K 21, 22, 26, 27, 30 (K 26)
	Symbol Name:	SY(**SOUNDG28**)
	Symbol Number:	**264**
	Symbol Explanation:	For deep soundings, greater than safety depth
	S57/INT1	SOUNDG I 2, 4, 10-15; K 17 (I 4)
		OBSTRN I 2, 4; K 41, 42, 46.2; L 20, 21.2; M 43; Q 42 (K 41)
		UWTROC K 11, 12, 14.1, 14.2,15; O 27 (K 14.1)
		WRECKS K 21, 22, 26, 27, 30 (K 26)
	Symbol Name:	SY(**SOUNDG29**)
	Symbol Number:	**265**
	Symbol Explanation:	For deep soundings, greater than safety depth
	S57/INT1	SOUNDG I 2, 4, 10-15; K 17 (I 4)
		OBSTRN I 2, 4; K 41, 42, 46.2; L 20, 21.2; M 43; Q 42 (K 41)
		UWTROC K 11, 12, 14.1, 14.2,15; O 27 (K 14.1)
		WRECKS K 21, 22, 26, 27, 30 (K 26)

	Symbol Name:	SY(**SOUNDG30**)	
	Symbol Number:	**266**	
	Symbol Explanation:	For deep soundings, greater than safety depth	
	S57/INT1	SOUNDG I 2, 4, 10-15; K 17 (I 4)	
		OBSTRN I 2, 4; K 41, 42, 46.2; L 20, 21.2; M 43; Q 42 (K 41)	
		UWTROC K 11, 12, 14.1, 14.2,15; O 27 (K 14.1)	
		WRECKS K 21, 22, 26, 27, 30 (K 26)	

	Symbol Name:	SY(**SOUNDG31**)	
	Symbol Number:	**267**	
	Symbol Explanation:	For deep soundings, greater than safety depth	
	S57/INT1	SOUNDG I 2, 4, 10-15; K 17 (I 4)	
		OBSTRN I 2, 4; K 41, 42, 46.2; L 20, 21.2; M 43; Q 42 (K 41)	
		UWTROC K 11, 12, 14.1, 14.2,15; O 27 (K 14.1)	
		WRECKS K 21, 22, 26, 27, 30 (K 26)	

	Symbol Name:	SY(**SOUNDG32**)	
	Symbol Number:	**268**	
	Symbol Explanation:	For deep soundings, greater than safety depth	
	S57/INT1	SOUNDG I 2, 4, 10-15; K 17 (I 4)	
		OBSTRN I 2, 4; K 41, 42, 46.2; L 20, 21.2; M 43; Q 42 (K 41)	
		UWTROC K 11, 12, 14.1, 14.2,15; O 27 (K 14.1)	
		WRECKS K 21, 22, 26, 27, 30 (K 26)	

	Symbol Name:	SY(**SOUNDG33**)	
	Symbol Number:	**269**	
	Symbol Explanation:	For deep soundings, greater than safety depth	
	S57/INT1	SOUNDG I 2, 4, 10-15; K 17 (I 4)	
		OBSTRN I 2, 4; K 41, 42, 46.2; L 20, 21.2; M 43; Q 42 (K 41)	
		UWTROC K 11, 12, 14.1, 14.2,15; O 27 (K 14.1)	
		WRECKS K 21, 22, 26, 27, 30 (K 26)	

	Symbol Name:	SY(**SOUNDG34**)	
	Symbol Number:	**270**	
	Symbol Explanation:	For deep soundings, greater than safety depth	
	S57/INT1	SOUNDG I 2, 4, 10-15; K 17 (I 4)	
		OBSTRN I 2, 4; K 41, 42, 46.2; L 20, 21.2; M 43; Q 42 (K 41)	
		UWTROC K 11, 12, 14.1, 14.2,15; O 27 (K 14.1)	
		WRECKS K 21, 22, 26, 27, 30 (K 26)	

	Symbol Name:	SY(**SOUNDG35**)	
	Symbol Number:	**271**	
	Symbol Explanation:	For deep soundings, greater than safety depth	
	S57/INT1	SOUNDG I 2, 4, 10-15; K 17 (I 4)	
		OBSTRN I 2, 4; K 41, 42, 46.2; L 20, 21.2; M 43; Q 42 (K 41)	
		UWTROC K 11, 12, 14.1, 14.2,15; O 27 (K 14.1)	
		WRECKS K 21, 22, 26, 27, 30 (K 26)	

	Symbol Name:	SY(**SOUNDG36**)	
	Symbol Number:	**272**	
	Symbol Explanation:	For deep soundings, greater than safety depth	
	S57/INT1	SOUNDG I 2, 4, 10-15; K 17 (I 4)	
		OBSTRN I 2, 4; K 41, 42, 46.2; L 20, 21.2; M 43; Q 42 (K 41)	
		UWTROC K 11, 12, 14.1, 14.2,15; O 27 (K 14.1)	
		WRECKS K 21, 22, 26, 27, 30 (K 26)	

	Symbol Name:	SY(**SOUNDG37**)	
	Symbol Number:	**273**	
	Symbol Explanation:	For deep soundings, greater than safety depth	
	S57/INT1	SOUNDG I 2, 4, 10-15; K 17 (I 4)	
		OBSTRN I 2, 4; K 41, 42, 46.2; L 20, 21.2; M 43; Q 42 (K 41)	
		UWTROC K 11, 12, 14.1, 14.2,15; O 27 (K 14.1)	
		WRECKS K 21, 22, 26, 27, 30 (K 26)	

	Symbol Name:	SY(**SOUNDG38**)
	Symbol Number:	**274**
	Symbol Explanation:	For deep soundings, greater than safety depth
	S57/INT1	SOUNDG I 2, 4, 10-15; K 17 (I 4)
		OBSTRN I 2, 4; K 41, 42, 46.2; L 20, 21.2; M 43; Q 42 (K 41)
		UWTROC K 11, 12, 14.1, 14.2,15; O 27 (K 14.1)
		WRECKS K 21, 22, 26, 27, 30 (K 26)

	Symbol Name:	SY(**SOUNDG39**)
	Symbol Number:	**275**
	Symbol Explanation:	For deep soundings, greater than safety depth
	S57/INT1	SOUNDG I 2, 4, 10-15; K 17 (I 4)
		OBSTRN I 2, 4; K 41, 42, 46.2; L 20, 21.2; M 43; Q 42 (K 41)
		UWTROC K 11, 12, 14.1, 14.2,15; O 27 (K 14.1)
		WRECKS K 21, 22, 26, 27, 30 (K 26)

	Symbol Name:	SY(**SOUNDG40**)
	Symbol Number:	**276**
	Symbol Explanation:	For deep soundings, greater than safety depth
	S57/INT1	SOUNDG I 2, 4, 10-15; K 17 (I 4)
		OBSTRN I 2, 4; K 41, 42, 46.2; L 20, 21.2; M 43; Q 42 (K 41)
		UWTROC K 11, 12, 14.1, 14.2,15; O 27 (K 14.1)
		WRECKS K 21, 22, 26, 27, 30 (K 26)

	Symbol Name:	SY(**SOUNDG41**)
	Symbol Number:	**277**
	Symbol Explanation:	For deep soundings, greater than safety depth
	S57/INT1	SOUNDG I 2, 4, 10-15; K 17 (I 4)
		OBSTRN I 2, 4; K 41, 42, 46.2; L 20, 21.2; M 43; Q 42 (K 41)
		UWTROC K 11, 12, 14.1, 14.2,15; O 27 (K 14.1)
		WRECKS K 21, 22, 26, 27, 30 (K 26)

	Symbol Name:	SY(**SOUNDG42**)
	Symbol Number:	**278**
	Symbol Explanation:	For deep soundings, greater than safety depth
	S57/INT1	SOUNDG I 2, 4, 10-15; K 17 (I 4)
		OBSTRN I 2, 4; K 41, 42, 46.2; L 20, 21.2; M 43; Q 42 (K 41)
		UWTROC K 11, 12, 14.1, 14.2,15; O 27 (K 14.1)
		WRECKS K 21, 22, 26, 27, 30 (K 26)

	Symbol Name:	SY(**SOUNDG43**)
	Symbol Number:	**279**
	Symbol Explanation:	For deep soundings, greater than safety depth
	S57/INT1	SOUNDG I 2, 4, 10-15; K 17 (I 4)
		OBSTRN I 2, 4; K 41, 42, 46.2; L 20, 21.2; M 43; Q 42 (K 41)
		UWTROC K 11, 12, 14.1, 14.2,15; O 27 (K 14.1)
		WRECKS K 21, 22, 26, 27, 30 (K 26)

	Symbol Name:	SY(**SOUNDG44**)
	Symbol Number:	**280**
	Symbol Explanation:	For deep soundings, greater than safety depth
	S57/INT1	SOUNDG I 2, 4, 10-15; K 17 (I 4)
		OBSTRN I 2, 4; K 41, 42, 46.2; L 20, 21.2; M 43; Q 42 (K 41)
		UWTROC K 11, 12, 14.1, 14.2,15; O 27 (K 14.1)
		WRECKS K 21, 22, 26, 27, 30 (K 26)

	Symbol Name:	SY(**SOUNDG45**)
	Symbol Number:	**281**
	Symbol Explanation:	For deep soundings, greater than safety depth
	S57/INT1	SOUNDG I 2, 4, 10-15; K 17 (I 4)
		OBSTRN I 2, 4; K 41, 42, 46.2; L 20, 21.2; M 43; Q 42 (K 41)
		UWTROC K 11, 12, 14.1, 14.2,15; O 27 (K 14.1)
		WRECKS K 21, 22, 26, 27, 30 (K 26)

Symbol Name:	SY(**SOUNDG46**)
Symbol Number:	**282**
Symbol Explanation:	For deep soundings, greater than safety depth
S57/INT1	SOUNDG I 2, 4, 10-15; K 17 (I 4)
	OBSTRN I 2, 4; K 41, 42, 46.2; L 20, 21.2; M 43; Q 42 (K 41)
	UWTROC K 11, 12, 14.1, 14.2,15; O 27 (K 14.1)
	WRECKS K 21, 22, 26, 27, 30 (K 26)

Symbol Name:	SY(**SOUNDG47**)
Symbol Number:	**283**
Symbol Explanation:	For deep soundings, greater than safety depth
S57/INT1	SOUNDG I 2, 4, 10-15; K 17 (I 4)
	OBSTRN I 2, 4; K 41, 42, 46.2; L 20, 21.2; M 43; Q 42 (K 41)
	UWTROC K 11, 12, 14.1, 14.2,15; O 27 (K 14.1)
	WRECKS K 21, 22, 26, 27, 30 (K 26)

Symbol Name:	SY(**SOUNDG48**)
Symbol Number:	**284**
Symbol Explanation:	For deep soundings, greater than safety depth
S57/INT1	SOUNDG I 2, 4, 10-15; K 17 (I 4)
	OBSTRN I 2, 4; K 41, 42, 46.2; L 20, 21.2; M 43; Q 42 (K 41)
	UWTROC K 11, 12, 14.1, 14.2,15; O 27 (K 14.1)
	WRECKS K 21, 22, 26, 27, 30 (K 26)

Symbol Name:	SY(**SOUNDG49**)
Symbol Number:	**285**
Symbol Explanation:	For deep soundings, greater than safety depth
S57/INT1	SOUNDG I 2, 4, 10-15; K 17 (I 4)
	OBSTRN I 2, 4; K 41, 42, 46.2; L 20, 21.2; M 43; Q 42 (K 41)
	UWTROC K 11, 12, 14.1, 14.2,15; O 27 (K 14.1)
	WRECKS K 21, 22, 26, 27, 30 (K 26)

Symbol Name:	SY(**SOUNDG50**)
Symbol Number:	**286**
Symbol Explanation:	For deep soundings, greater than safety depth
S57/INT1	SOUNDG I 2, 4, 10-15; K 17 (I 4)
	OBSTRN I 2, 4; K 41, 42, 46.2; L 20, 21.2; M 43; Q 42 (K 41)
	UWTROC K 11, 12, 14.1, 14.2,15; O 27 (K 14.1)
	WRECKS K 21, 22, 26, 27, 30 (K 26)

Symbol Name:	SY(**SOUNDG51**)
Symbol Number:	**287**
Symbol Explanation:	For deep soundings, greater than safety depth
S57/INT1	SOUNDG I 2, 4, 10-15; K 17 (I 4)
	OBSTRN I 2, 4; K 41, 42, 46.2; L 20, 21.2; M 43; Q 42 (K 41)
	UWTROC K 11, 12, 14.1, 14.2,15; O 27 (K 14.1)
	WRECKS K 21, 22, 26, 27, 30 (K 26)

Symbol Name:	SY(**SOUNDG52**)
Symbol Number:	**288**
Symbol Explanation:	For deep soundings, greater than safety depth
S57/INT1	SOUNDG I 2, 4, 10-15; K 17 (I 4)
	OBSTRN I 2, 4; K 41, 42, 46.2; L 20, 21.2; M 43; Q 42 (K 41)
	UWTROC K 11, 12, 14.1, 14.2,15; O 27 (K 14.1)
	WRECKS K 21, 22, 26, 27, 30 (K 26)

Symbol Name:	SY(**SOUNDG53**)
Symbol Number:	**289**
Symbol Explanation:	For deep soundings, greater than safety depth
S57/INT1	SOUNDG I 2, 4, 10-15; K 17 (I 4)
	OBSTRN I 2, 4; K 41, 42, 46.2; L 20, 21.2; M 43; Q 42 (K 41)
	UWTROC K 11, 12, 14.1, 14.2,15; O 27 (K 14.1)
	WRECKS K 21, 22, 26, 27, 30 (K 26)

	Symbol Name:	SY(**SOUNDG54**)
	Symbol Number:	**290**
	Symbol Explanation:	For deep soundings, greater than safety depth
	S57/INT1	SOUNDG I 2, 4, 10-15; K 17 (I 4)
		OBSTRN I 2, 4; K 41, 42, 46.2; L 20, 21.2; M 43; Q 42 (K 41)
		UWTROC K 11, 12, 14.1, 14.2,15; O 27 (K 14.1)
		WRECKS K 21, 22, 26, 27, 30 (K 26)
	Symbol Name:	SY(**SOUNDG55**)
	Symbol Number:	**291**
	Symbol Explanation:	For deep soundings, greater than safety depth
	S57/INT1	SOUNDG I 2, 4, 10-15; K 17 (I 4)
		OBSTRN I 2, 4; K 41, 42, 46.2; L 20, 21.2; M 43; Q 42 (K 41)
		UWTROC K 11, 12, 14.1, 14.2,15; O 27 (K 14.1)
		WRECKS K 21, 22, 26, 27, 30 (K 26)
	Symbol Name:	SY(**SOUNDG56**)
	Symbol Number:	**292**
	Symbol Explanation:	For deep soundings, greater than safety depth
	S57/INT1	SOUNDG I 2, 4, 10-15; K 17 (I 4)
		OBSTRN I 2, 4; K 41, 42, 46.2; L 20, 21.2; M 43; Q 42 (K 41)
		UWTROC K 11, 12, 14.1, 14.2,15; O 27 (K 14.1)
		WRECKS K 21, 22, 26, 27, 30 (K 26)
	Symbol Name:	SY(**SOUNDG57**)
	Symbol Number:	**293**
	Symbol Explanation:	For deep soundings, greater than safety depth
	S57/INT1	SOUNDG I 2, 4, 10-15; K 17 (I 4)
		OBSTRN I 2, 4; K 41, 42, 46.2; L 20, 21.2; M 43; Q 42 (K 41)
		UWTROC K 11, 12, 14.1, 14.2,15; O 27 (K 14.1)
		WRECKS K 21, 22, 26, 27, 30 (K 26)
	Symbol Name:	SY(**SOUNDG58**)
	Symbol Number:	**294**
	Symbol Explanation:	For deep soundings, greater than safety depth
	S57/INT1	SOUNDG I 2, 4, 10-15; K 17 (I 4)
		OBSTRN I 2, 4; K 41, 42, 46.2; L 20, 21.2; M 43; Q 42 (K 41)
		UWTROC K 11, 12, 14.1, 14.2,15; O 27 (K 14.1)
		WRECKS K 21, 22, 26, 27, 30 (K 26)
	Symbol Name:	SY(**SOUNDG59**)
	Symbol Number:	**295**
	Symbol Explanation:	For deep soundings, greater than safety depth
	S57/INT1	SOUNDG I 2, 4, 10-15; K 17 (I 4)
		OBSTRN I 2, 4; K 41, 42, 46.2; L 20, 21.2; M 43; Q 42 (K 41)
		UWTROC K 11, 12, 14.1, 14.2,15; O 27 (K 14.1)
		WRECKS K 21, 22, 26, 27, 30 (K 26)
	Symbol Name:	SY(**SOUNDGB1**)
	Symbol Number:	**296**
	Symbol Explanation:	Symbol for swept sounding, used for deep soundings greater than safety depth
	S57/INT1	As applicable K 2
		OBSTRN K 42
		WRECKS K 27
	Symbol Name:	SY(**SOUNDGC2**)
	Symbol Number:	**298**
	Symbol Explanation:	Sounding of low accuracy
	S57/INT1	As applicable B 7, 8; I 1, 3.1, 3.2; IP 89 (B 8)
		OBSTRN I 2 (I 2)
		SOUNDG I 2, 4, 13, 14 (I 14)

Symbol Name:	SY(**SOUNDS00**)	
Symbol Number:	**299**	
Symbol Explanation:	Shallow soundings, less than or equal to the safety depth	
S57/INT1	SOUNDG I 2, 4, 10-15; K 17 (I 10)	
	OBSTRN I 2, 4; K 41, 42, 46.2; L 20, 21.2; M 43; Q 42 (L 21.2)	
	UWTROC K 11, 12, 14.1, 14.2, 15; O 27 (K 15)	
	WRECKS K 21, 22, 26, 27, 30 (K 30)	

Symbol Name:	SY(**SOUNDS01**)	
Symbol Number:	**300**	
Symbol Explanation:	Shallow soundings, less than or equal to the safety depth	
S57/INT1	SOUNDG I 2, 4, 10-15; K 17 (I 10)	
	OBSTRN I 2, 4; K 41, 42, 46.2; L 20, 21.2; M 43; Q 42 (L 21.2)	
	UWTROC K 11, 12, 14.1, 14.2, 15; O 27 (K 15)	
	WRECKS K 21, 22, 26, 27, 30 (K 30)	

Symbol Name:	SY(**SOUNDS02**)	
Symbol Number:	**301**	
Symbol Explanation:	Shallow soundings, less than or equal to the safety depth	
S57/INT1	SOUNDG I 2, 4, 10-15; K 17 (I 10)	
	OBSTRN I 2, 4; K 41, 42, 46.2; L 20, 21.2; M 43; Q 42 (L 21.2)	
	UWTROC K 11, 12, 14.1, 14.2, 15; O 27 (K 15)	
	WRECKS K 21, 22, 26, 27, 30 (K 30)	

Symbol Name:	SY(**SOUNDS03**)	
Symbol Number:	**302**	
Symbol Explanation:	Shallow soundings, less than or equal to the safety depth	
S57/INT1	SOUNDG I 2, 4, 10-15; K 17 (I 10)	
	OBSTRN I 2, 4; K 41, 42, 46.2; L 20, 21.2; M 43; Q 42 (L 21.2)	
	UWTROC K 11, 12, 14.1, 14.2, 15; O 27 (K 15)	
	WRECKS K 21, 22, 26, 27, 30 (K 30)	

Symbol Name:	SY(**SOUNDS04**)	
Symbol Number:	**303**	
Symbol Explanation:	Shallow soundings, less than or equal to the safety depth	
S57/INT1	SOUNDG I 2, 4, 10-15; K 17 (I 10)	
	OBSTRN I 2, 4; K 41, 42, 46.2; L 20, 21.2; M 43; Q 42 (L 21.2)	
	UWTROC K 11, 12, 14.1, 14.2, 15; O 27 (K 15)	
	WRECKS K 21, 22, 26, 27, 30 (K 30)	

Symbol Name:	SY(**SOUNDS05**)	
Symbol Number:	**304**	
Symbol Explanation:	Shallow soundings, less than or equal to the safety depth	
S57/INT1	SOUNDG I 2, 4, 10-15; K 17 (I 10)	
	OBSTRN I 2, 4; K 41, 42, 46.2; L 20, 21.2; M 43; Q 42 (L 21.2)	
	UWTROC K 11, 12, 14.1, 14.2, 15; O 27 (K 15)	
	WRECKS K 21, 22, 26, 27, 30 (K 30)	

Symbol Name:	SY(**SOUNDS06**)	
Symbol Number:	**305**	
Symbol Explanation:	Shallow soundings, less than or equal to the safety depth	
S57/INT1	SOUNDG I 2, 4, 10-15; K 17 (I 10)	
	OBSTRN I 2, 4; K 41, 42, 46.2; L 20, 21.2; M 43; Q 42 (L 21.2)	
	UWTROC K 11, 12, 14.1, 14.2, 15; O 27 (K 15)	
	WRECKS K 21, 22, 26, 27, 30 (K 30)	

Symbol Name:	SY(**SOUNDS07**)	
Symbol Number:	**306**	
Symbol Explanation:	Shallow soundings, less than or equal to the safety depth	
S57/INT1	SOUNDG I 2, 4, 10-15; K 17 (I 10)	
	OBSTRN I 2, 4; K 41, 42, 46.2; L 20, 21.2; M 43; Q 42 (L 21.2)	
	UWTROC K 11, 12, 14.1, 14.2, 15; O 27 (K 15)	
	WRECKS K 21, 22, 26, 27, 30 (K 30)	

Symbol Name:	SY(**SOUNDS08**)	
Symbol Number:	**307**	
Symbol Explanation:	Shallow soundings, less than or equal to the safety depth	
S57/INT1	SOUNDG I 2, 4, 10-15; K 17 (I 10)	
	OBSTRN I 2, 4; K 41, 42, 46.2; L 20, 21.2; M 43; Q 42 (L 21.2)	
	UWTROC K 11, 12, 14.1, 14.2, 15; O 27 (K 15)	
	WRECKS K 21, 22, 26, 27, 30 (K 30)	
Symbol Name:	SY(**SOUNDS09**)	
Symbol Number:	**308**	
Symbol Explanation:	Shallow soundings, less than or equal to the safety depth	
S57/INT1	SOUNDG I 2, 4, 10-15; K 17 (I 10)	
	OBSTRN I 2, 4; K 41, 42, 46.2; L 20, 21.2; M 43; Q 42 (L 21.2)	
	UWTROC K 11, 12, 14.1, 14.2, 15; O 27 (K 15)	
	WRECKS K 21, 22, 26, 27, 30 (K 30)	
Symbol Name:	SY(**SOUNDS10**)	
Symbol Number:	**309**	
Symbol Explanation:	Shallow soundings, less than or equal to the safety depth	
S57/INT1	SOUNDG I 2, 4, 10-15; K 17 (I 10)	
	OBSTRN I 2, 4; K 41, 42, 46.2; L 20, 21.2; M 43; Q 42 (L 21.2)	
	UWTROC K 11, 12, 14.1, 14.2, 15; O 27 (K 15)	
	WRECKS K 21, 22, 26, 27, 30 (K 30)	
Symbol Name:	SY(**SOUNDS11**)	
Symbol Number:	**310**	
Symbol Explanation:	Shallow soundings, less than or equal to the safety depth	
S57/INT1	SOUNDG I 2, 4, 10-15; K 17 (I 10)	
	OBSTRN I 2, 4; K 41, 42, 46.2; L 20, 21.2; M 43; Q 42 (L 21.2)	
	UWTROC K 11, 12, 14.1, 14.2, 15; O 27 (K 15)	
	WRECKS K 21, 22, 26, 27, 30 (K 30)	
Symbol Name:	SY(**SOUNDS12**)	
Symbol Number:	**311**	
Symbol Explanation:	Shallow soundings, less than or equal to the safety depth	
S57/INT1	SOUNDG I 2, 4, 10-15; K 17 (I 10)	
	OBSTRN I 2, 4; K 41, 42, 46.2; L 20, 21.2; M 43; Q 42 (L 21.2)	
	UWTROC K 11, 12, 14.1, 14.2, 15; O 27 (K 15)	
	WRECKS K 21, 22, 26, 27, 30 (K 30)	
Symbol Name:	SY(**SOUNDS13**)	
Symbol Number:	**312**	
Symbol Explanation:	Shallow soundings, less than or equal to the safety depth	
S57/INT1	SOUNDG I 2, 4, 10-15; K 17 (I 10)	
	OBSTRN I 2, 4; K 41, 42, 46.2; L 20, 21.2; M 43; Q 42 (L 21.2)	
	UWTROC K 11, 12, 14.1, 14.2, 15; O 27 (K 15)	
	WRECKS K 21, 22, 26, 27, 30 (K 30)	
Symbol Name:	SY(**SOUNDS14**)	
Symbol Number:	**313**	
Symbol Explanation:	Shallow soundings, less than or equal to the safety depth	
S57/INT1	SOUNDG I 2, 4, 10-15; K 17 (I 10)	
	OBSTRN I 2, 4; K 41, 42, 46.2; L 20, 21.2; M 43; Q 42 (L 21.2)	
	UWTROC K 11, 12, 14.1, 14.2, 15; O 27 (K 15)	
	WRECKS K 21, 22, 26, 27, 30 (K 30)	
Symbol Name:	SY(**SOUNDS15**)	
Symbol Number:	**314**	
Symbol Explanation:	Shallow soundings, less than or equal to the safety depth	
S57/INT1	SOUNDG I 2, 4, 10-15; K 17 (I 10)	
	OBSTRN I 2, 4; K 41, 42, 46.2; L 20, 21.2; M 43; Q 42 (L 21.2)	
	UWTROC K 11, 12, 14.1, 14.2, 15; O 27 (K 15)	
	WRECKS K 21, 22, 26, 27, 30 (K 30)	

Symbol Name:	SY(**SOUNDS16**)	
Symbol Number:	**315**	
Symbol Explanation:	Shallow soundings, less than or equal to the safety depth	
S57/INT1	SOUNDG I 2, 4, 10-15; K 17 (I 10)	
	OBSTRN I 2, 4; K 41, 42, 46.2; L 20, 21.2; M 43; Q 42 (L 21.2)	
	UWTROC K 11, 12, 14.1, 14.2, 15; O 27 (K 15)	
	WRECKS K 21, 22, 26, 27, 30 (K 30)	

Symbol Name:	SY(**SOUNDS17**)	
Symbol Number:	**316**	
Symbol Explanation:	Shallow soundings, less than or equal to the safety depth	
S57/INT1	SOUNDG I 2, 4, 10-15; K 17 (I 10)	
	OBSTRN I 2, 4; K 41, 42, 46.2; L 20, 21.2; M 43; Q 42 (L 21.2)	
	UWTROC K 11, 12, 14.1, 14.2, 15; O 27 (K 15)	
	WRECKS K 21, 22, 26, 27, 30 (K 30)	

Symbol Name:	SY(**SOUNDS18**)	
Symbol Number:	**317**	
Symbol Explanation:	Shallow soundings, less than or equal to the safety depth	
S57/INT1	SOUNDG I 2, 4, 10-15; K 17 (I 10)	
	OBSTRN I 2, 4; K 41, 42, 46.2; L 20, 21.2; M 43; Q 42 (L 21.2)	
	UWTROC K 11, 12, 14.1, 14.2, 15; O 27 (K 15)	
	WRECKS K 21, 22, 26, 27, 30 (K 30)	

Symbol Name:	SY(**SOUNDS19**)	
Symbol Number:	**318**	
Symbol Explanation:	Shallow soundings, less than or equal to the safety depth	
S57/INT1	SOUNDG I 2, 4, 10-15; K 17 (I 10)	
	OBSTRN I 2, 4; K 41, 42, 46.2; L 20, 21.2; M 43; Q 42 (L 21.2)	
	UWTROC K 11, 12, 14.1, 14.2, 15; O 27 (K 15)	
	WRECKS K 21, 22, 26, 27, 30 (K 30)	

Symbol Name:	SY(**SOUNDS20**)	
Symbol Number:	**319**	
Symbol Explanation:	Shallow soundings, less than or equal to the safety depth	
S57/INT1	SOUNDG I 2, 4, 10-15; K 17 (I 10)	
	OBSTRN I 2, 4; K 41, 42, 46.2; L 20, 21.2; M 43; Q 42 (L 21.2)	
	UWTROC K 11, 12, 14.1, 14.2, 15; O 27 (K 15)	
	WRECKS K 21, 22, 26, 27, 30 (K 30)	

Symbol Name:	SY(**SOUNDS21**)	
Symbol Number:	**320**	
Symbol Explanation:	Shallow soundings, less than or equal to the safety depth	
S57/INT1	SOUNDG I 2, 4, 10-15; K 17 (I 10)	
	OBSTRN I 2, 4; K 41, 42, 46.2; L 20, 21.2; M 43; Q 42 (L 21.2)	
	UWTROC K 11, 12, 14.1, 14.2, 15; O 27 (K 15)	
	WRECKS K 21, 22, 26, 27, 30 (K 30)	

Symbol Name:	SY(**SOUNDS22**)	
Symbol Number:	**321**	
Symbol Explanation:	Shallow soundings, less than or equal to the safety depth	
S57/INT1	SOUNDG I 2, 4, 10-15; K 17 (I 10)	
	OBSTRN I 2, 4; K 41, 42, 46.2; L 20, 21.2; M 43; Q 42 (L 21.2)	
	UWTROC K 11, 12, 14.1, 14.2, 15; O 27 (K 15)	
	WRECKS K 21, 22, 26, 27, 30 (K 30)	

Symbol Name:	SY(**SOUNDS23**)	
Symbol Number:	**322**	
Symbol Explanation:	Shallow soundings, less than or equal to the safety depth	
S57/INT1	SOUNDG I 2, 4, 10-15; K 17 (I 10)	
	OBSTRN I 2, 4; K 41, 42, 46.2; L 20, 21.2; M 43; Q 42 (L 21.2)	
	UWTROC K 11, 12, 14.1, 14.2, 15; O 27 (K 15)	
	WRECKS K 21, 22, 26, 27, 30 (K 30)	

		Symbol Name:	SY(**SOUNDS24**)
		Symbol Number:	**323**
		Symbol Explanation:	Shallow soundings, less than or equal to the safety depth
		S57/INT1	SOUNDG I 2, 4, 10-15; K 17 (I 10)
			OBSTRN I 2, 4; K 41, 42, 46.2; L 20, 21.2; M 43; Q 42 (L 21.2)
			UWTROC K 11, 12, 14.1, 14.2, 15; O 27 (K 15)
			WRECKS K 21, 22, 26, 27, 30 (K 30)
		Symbol Name:	SY(**SOUNDS25**)
		Symbol Number:	**324**
		Symbol Explanation:	Shallow soundings, less than or equal to the safety depth
		S57/INT1	SOUNDG I 2, 4, 10-15; K 17 (I 10)
			OBSTRN I 2, 4; K 41, 42, 46.2; L 20, 21.2; M 43; Q 42 (L 21.2)
			UWTROC K 11, 12, 14.1, 14.2, 15; O 27 (K 15)
			WRECKS K 21, 22, 26, 27, 30 (K 30)
		Symbol Name:	SY(**SOUNDS26**)
		Symbol Number:	**325**
		Symbol Explanation:	Shallow soundings, less than or equal to the safety depth
		S57/INT1	SOUNDG I 2, 4, 10-15; K 17 (I 10)
			OBSTRN I 2, 4; K 41, 42, 46.2; L 20, 21.2; M 43; Q 42 (L 21.2)
			UWTROC K 11, 12, 14.1, 14.2, 15; O 27 (K 15)
			WRECKS K 21, 22, 26, 27, 30 (K 30)
		Symbol Name:	SY(**SOUNDS27**)
		Symbol Number:	**326**
		Symbol Explanation:	Shallow soundings, less than or equal to the safety depth
		S57/INT1	SOUNDG I 2, 4, 10-15; K 17 (I 10)
			OBSTRN I 2, 4; K 41, 42, 46.2; L 20, 21.2; M 43; Q 42 (L 21.2)
			UWTROC K 11, 12, 14.1, 14.2, 15; O 27 (K 15)
			WRECKS K 21, 22, 26, 27, 30 (K 30)
		Symbol Name:	SY(**SOUNDS28**)
		Symbol Number:	**327**
		Symbol Explanation:	Shallow soundings, less than or equal to the safety depth
		S57/INT1	SOUNDG I 2, 4, 10-15; K 17 (I 10)
			OBSTRN I 2, 4; K 41, 42, 46.2; L 20, 21.2; M 43; Q 42 (L 21.2)
			UWTROC K 11, 12, 14.1, 14.2, 15; O 27 (K 15)
			WRECKS K 21, 22, 26, 27, 30 (K 30)
		Symbol Name:	SY(**SOUNDS29**)
		Symbol Number:	**328**
		Symbol Explanation:	Shallow soundings, less than or equal to the safety depth
		S57/INT1	SOUNDG I 2, 4, 10-15; K 17 (I 10)
			OBSTRN I 2, 4; K 41, 42, 46.2; L 20, 21.2; M 43; Q 42 (L 21.2)
			UWTROC K 11, 12, 14.1, 14.2, 15; O 27 (K 15)
			WRECKS K 21, 22, 26, 27, 30 (K 30)
		Symbol Name:	SY(**SOUNDS30**)
		Symbol Number:	**329**
		Symbol Explanation:	Shallow soundings, less than or equal to the safety depth
		S57/INT1	SOUNDG I 2, 4, 10-15; K 17 (I 10)
			OBSTRN I 2, 4; K 41, 42, 46.2; L 20, 21.2; M 43; Q 42 (L 21.2)
			UWTROC K 11, 12, 14.1, 14.2, 15; O 27 (K 15)
			WRECKS K 21, 22, 26, 27, 30 (K 30)
		Symbol Name:	SY(**SOUNDS31**)
		Symbol Number:	**330**
		Symbol Explanation:	Shallow soundings, less than or equal to the safety depth
		S57/INT1	SOUNDG I 2, 4, 10-15; K 17 (I 10)
			OBSTRN I 2, 4; K 41, 42, 46.2; L 20, 21.2; M 43; Q 42 (L 21.2)
			UWTROC K 11, 12, 14.1, 14.2, 15; O 27 (K 15)
			WRECKS K 21, 22, 26, 27, 30 (K 30)

2		**Symbol Name:**	SY(**SOUNDS32**)
		Symbol Number:	**331**
		Symbol Explanation:	Shallow soundings, less than or equal to the safety depth
		S57/INT1	SOUNDG I 2, 4, 10-15; K 17 (I 10) OBSTRN I 2, 4; K 41, 42, 46.2; L 20, 21.2; M 43; Q 42 (L 21.2) UWTROC K 11, 12, 14.1, 14.2, 15; O 27 (K 15) WRECKS K 21, 22, 26, 27, 30 (K 30)
3		**Symbol Name:**	SY(**SOUNDS33**)
		Symbol Number:	**332**
		Symbol Explanation:	Shallow soundings, less than or equal to the safety depth
		S57/INT1	SOUNDG I 2, 4, 10-15; K 17 (I 10) OBSTRN I 2, 4; K 41, 42, 46.2; L 20, 21.2; M 43; Q 42 (L 21.2) UWTROC K 11, 12, 14.1, 14.2, 15; O 27 (K 15) WRECKS K 21, 22, 26, 27, 30 (K 30)
4		**Symbol Name:**	SY(**SOUNDS34**)
		Symbol Number:	**333**
		Symbol Explanation:	Shallow soundings, less than or equal to the safety depth
		S57/INT1	SOUNDG I 2, 4, 10-15; K 17 (I 10) OBSTRN I 2, 4; K 41, 42, 46.2; L 20, 21.2; M 43; Q 42 (L 21.2) UWTROC K 11, 12, 14.1, 14.2, 15; O 27 (K 15) WRECKS K 21, 22, 26, 27, 30 (K 30)
5		**Symbol Name:**	SY(**SOUNDS35**)
		Symbol Number:	**334**
		Symbol Explanation:	Shallow soundings, less than or equal to the safety depth
		S57/INT1	SOUNDG I 2, 4, 10-15; K 17 (I 10) OBSTRN I 2, 4; K 41, 42, 46.2; L 20, 21.2; M 43; Q 42 (L 21.2) UWTROC K 11, 12, 14.1, 14.2, 15; O 27 (K 15) WRECKS K 21, 22, 26, 27, 30 (K 30)
6		**Symbol Name:**	SY(**SOUNDS36**)
		Symbol Number:	**335**
		Symbol Explanation:	Shallow soundings, less than or equal to the safety depth
		S57/INT1	SOUNDG I 2, 4, 10-15; K 17 (I 10) OBSTRN I 2, 4; K 41, 42, 46.2; L 20, 21.2; M 43; Q 42 (L 21.2) UWTROC K 11, 12, 14.1, 14.2, 15; O 27 (K 15) WRECKS K 21, 22, 26, 27, 30 (K 30)
7		**Symbol Name:**	SY(**SOUNDS37**)
		Symbol Number:	**336**
		Symbol Explanation:	Shallow soundings, less than or equal to the safety depth
		S57/INT1	SOUNDG I 2, 4, 10-15; K 17 (I 10) OBSTRN I 2, 4; K 41, 42, 46.2; L 20, 21.2; M 43; Q 42 (L 21.2) UWTROC K 11, 12, 14.1, 14.2, 15; O 27 (K 15) WRECKS K 21, 22, 26, 27, 30 (K 30)
8		**Symbol Name:**	SY(**SOUNDS38**)
		Symbol Number:	**337**
		Symbol Explanation:	Shallow soundings, less than or equal to the safety depth
		S57/INT1	SOUNDG I 2, 4, 10-15; K 17 (I 10) OBSTRN I 2, 4; K 41, 42, 46.2; L 20, 21.2; M 43; Q 42 (L 21.2) UWTROC K 11, 12, 14.1, 14.2, 15; O 27 (K 15) WRECKS K 21, 22, 26, 27, 30 (K 30)
9		**Symbol Name:**	SY(**SOUNDS39**)
		Symbol Number:	**338**
		Symbol Explanation:	Shallow soundings, less than or equal to the safety depth
		S57/INT1	SOUNDG I 2, 4, 10-15; K 17 (I 10) OBSTRN I 2, 4; K 41, 42, 46.2; L 20, 21.2; M 43; Q 42 (L 21.2) UWTROC K 11, 12, 14.1, 14.2, 15; O 27 (K 15) WRECKS K 21, 22, 26, 27, 30 (K 30)

	Symbol Name: SY(**SOUNDS40**) **Symbol Number:** 339 **Symbol Explanation:** Shallow soundings, less than or equal to the safety depth **S57/INT1** SOUNDG I 2, 4, 10-15; K 17 (I 10) OBSTRN I 2, 4; K 41, 42, 46.2; L 20, 21.2; M 43; Q 42 (L 21.2) UWTROC K 11, 12, 14.1, 14.2, 15; O 27 (K 15) WRECKS K 21, 22, 26, 27, 30 (K 30)
	Symbol Name: SY(**SOUNDS41**) **Symbol Number:** 340 **Symbol Explanation:** Shallow soundings, less than or equal to the safety depth **S57/INT1** SOUNDG I 2, 4, 10-15; K 17 (I 10) OBSTRN I 2, 4; K 41, 42, 46.2; L 20, 21.2; M 43; Q 42 (L 21.2) UWTROC K 11, 12, 14.1, 14.2, 15; O 27 (K 15) WRECKS K 21, 22, 26, 27, 30 (K 30)
	Symbol Name: SY(**SOUNDS42**) **Symbol Number:** 341 **Symbol Explanation:** Shallow soundings, less than or equal to the safety depth **S57/INT1** SOUNDG I 2, 4, 10-15; K 17 (I 10) OBSTRN I 2, 4; K 41, 42, 46.2; L 20, 21.2; M 43; Q 42 (L 21.2) UWTROC K 11, 12, 14.1, 14.2, 15; O 27 (K 15) WRECKS K 21, 22, 26, 27, 30 (K 30)
	Symbol Name: SY(**SOUNDS43**) **Symbol Number:** 342 **Symbol Explanation:** Shallow soundings, less than or equal to the safety depth **S57/INT1** SOUNDG I 2, 4, 10-15; K 17 (I 10) OBSTRN I 2, 4; K 41, 42, 46.2; L 20, 21.2; M 43; Q 42 (L 21.2) UWTROC K 11, 12, 14.1, 14.2, 15; O 27 (K 15) WRECKS K 21, 22, 26, 27, 30 (K 30)
	Symbol Name: SY(**SOUNDS44**) **Symbol Number:** 343 **Symbol Explanation:** Shallow soundings, less than or equal to the safety depth **S57/INT1** SOUNDG I 2, 4, 10-15; K 17 (I 10) OBSTRN I 2, 4; K 41, 42, 46.2; L 20, 21.2; M 43; Q 42 (L 21.2) UWTROC K 11, 12, 14.1, 14.2, 15; O 27 (K 15) WRECKS K 21, 22, 26, 27, 30 (K 30)
	Symbol Name: SY(**SOUNDS45**) **Symbol Number:** 344 **Symbol Explanation:** Shallow soundings, less than or equal to the safety depth **S57/INT1** SOUNDG I 2, 4, 10-15; K 17 (I 10) OBSTRN I 2, 4; K 41, 42, 46.2; L 20, 21.2; M 43; Q 42 (L 21.2) UWTROC K 11, 12, 14.1, 14.2, 15; O 27 (K 15) WRECKS K 21, 22, 26, 27, 30 (K 30)
	Symbol Name: SY(**SOUNDS46**) **Symbol Number:** 345 **Symbol Explanation:** Shallow soundings, less than or equal to the safety depth **S57/INT1** SOUNDG I 2, 4, 10-15; K 17 (I 10) OBSTRN I 2, 4; K 41, 42, 46.2; L 20, 21.2; M 43; Q 42 (L 21.2) UWTROC K 11, 12, 14.1, 14.2, 15; O 27 (K 15) WRECKS K 21, 22, 26, 27, 30 (K 30)
	Symbol Name: SY(**SOUNDS47**) **Symbol Number:** 346 **Symbol Explanation:** Shallow soundings, less than or equal to the safety depth **S57/INT1** SOUNDG I 2, 4, 10-15; K 17 (I 10) OBSTRN I 2, 4; K 41, 42, 46.2; L 20, 21.2; M 43; Q 42 (L 21.2) UWTROC K 11, 12, 14.1, 14.2, 15; O 27 (K 15) WRECKS K 21, 22, 26, 27, 30 (K 30)

Symbol Name:	SY(**SOUNDS48**)
Symbol Number:	**347**
Symbol Explanation:	Shallow soundings, less than or equal to the safety depth
S57/INT1	SOUNDG I 2, 4, 10-15; K 17 (I 10)
	OBSTRN I 2, 4; K 41, 42, 46.2; L 20, 21.2; M 43; Q 42 (L 21.2)
	UWTROC K 11, 12, 14.1, 14.2, 15; O 27 (K 15)
	WRECKS K 21, 22, 26, 27, 30 (K 30)

Symbol Name:	SY(**SOUNDS49**)
Symbol Number:	**348**
Symbol Explanation:	Shallow soundings, less than or equal to the safety depth
S57/INT1	SOUNDG I 2, 4, 10-15; K 17 (I 10)
	OBSTRN I 2, 4; K 41, 42, 46.2; L 20, 21.2; M 43; Q 42 (L 21.2)
	UWTROC K 11, 12, 14.1, 14.2, 15; O 27 (K 15)
	WRECKS K 21, 22, 26, 27, 30 (K 30)

Symbol Name:	SY(**SOUNDS50**)
Symbol Number:	**349**
Symbol Explanation:	Shallow soundings, less than or equal to the safety depth
S57/INT1	SOUNDG I 2, 4, 10-15; K 17 (I 10)
	OBSTRN I 2, 4; K 41, 42, 46.2; L 20, 21.2; M 43; Q 42 (L 21.2)
	UWTROC K 11, 12, 14.1, 14.2, 15; O 27 (K 15)
	WRECKS K 21, 22, 26, 27, 30 (K 30)

Symbol Name:	SY(**SOUNDS51**)
Symbol Number:	**350**
Symbol Explanation:	Shallow soundings, less than or equal to the safety depth
S57/INT1	SOUNDG I 2, 4, 10-15; K 17 (I 10)
	OBSTRN I 2, 4; K 41, 42, 46.2; L 20, 21.2; M 43; Q 42 (L 21.2)
	UWTROC K 11, 12, 14.1, 14.2, 15; O 27 (K 15)
	WRECKS K 21, 22, 26, 27, 30 (K 30)

Symbol Name:	SY(**SOUNDS52**)
Symbol Number:	**351**
Symbol Explanation:	Shallow soundings, less than or equal to the safety depth
S57/INT1	SOUNDG I 2, 4, 10-15; K 17 (I 10)
	OBSTRN I 2, 4; K 41, 42, 46.2; L 20, 21.2; M 43; Q 42 (L 21.2)
	UWTROC K 11, 12, 14.1, 14.2, 15; O 27 (K 15)
	WRECKS K 21, 22, 26, 27, 30 (K 30)

Symbol Name:	SY(**SOUNDS53**)
Symbol Number:	**352**
Symbol Explanation:	Shallow soundings, less than or equal to the safety depth
S57/INT1	SOUNDG I 2, 4, 10-15; K 17 (I 10)
	OBSTRN I 2, 4; K 41, 42, 46.2; L 20, 21.2; M 43; Q 42 (L 21.2)
	UWTROC K 11, 12, 14.1, 14.2, 15; O 27 (K 15)
	WRECKS K 21, 22, 26, 27, 30 (K 30)

Symbol Name:	SY(**SOUNDS54**)
Symbol Number:	**353**
Symbol Explanation:	Shallow soundings, less than or equal to the safety depth
S57/INT1	SOUNDG I 2, 4, 10-15; K 17 (I 10)
	OBSTRN I 2, 4; K 41, 42, 46.2; L 20, 21.2; M 43; Q 42 (L 21.2)
	UWTROC K 11, 12, 14.1, 14.2, 15; O 27 (K 15)
	WRECKS K 21, 22, 26, 27, 30 (K 30)

Symbol Name:	SY(**SOUNDS55**)
Symbol Number:	**354**
Symbol Explanation:	Shallow soundings, less than or equal to the safety depth
S57/INT1	SOUNDG I 2, 4, 10-15; K 17 (I 10)
	OBSTRN I 2, 4; K 41, 42, 46.2; L 20, 21.2; M 43; Q 42 (L 21.2)
	UWTROC K 11, 12, 14.1, 14.2, 15; O 27 (K 15)
	WRECKS K 21, 22, 26, 27, 30 (K 30)

	Symbol Name:	SY(**SOUNDS56**)
	Symbol Number:	**355**
	Symbol Explanation:	Shallow soundings, less than or equal to the safety depth
	S57/INT1	SOUNDG I 2, 4, 10-15; K 17 (I 10) OBSTRN I 2, 4; K 41, 42, 46.2; L 20, 21.2; M 43; Q 42 (L 21.2) UWTROC K 11, 12, 14.1, 14.2, 15; O 27 (K 15) WRECKS K 21, 22, 26, 27, 30 (K 30)
	Symbol Name:	SY(**SOUNDS57**)
	Symbol Number:	**356**
	Symbol Explanation:	Shallow soundings, less than or equal to the safety depth
	S57/INT1	SOUNDG I 2, 4, 10-15; K 17 (I 10) OBSTRN I 2, 4; K 41, 42, 46.2; L 20, 21.2; M 43; Q 42 (L 21.2) UWTROC K 11, 12, 14.1, 14.2, 15; O 27 (K 15) WRECKS K 21, 22, 26, 27, 30 (K 30)
	Symbol Name:	SY(**SOUNDS58**)
	Symbol Number:	**357**
	Symbol Explanation:	Shallow soundings, less than or equal to the safety depth
	S57/INT1	SOUNDG I 2, 4, 10-15; K 17 (I 10) OBSTRN I 2, 4; K 41, 42, 46.2; L 20, 21.2; M 43; Q 42 (L 21.2) UWTROC K 11, 12, 14.1, 14.2, 15; O 27 (K 15) WRECKS K 21, 22, 26, 27, 30 (K 30)
	Symbol Name:	SY(**SOUNDS59**)
	Symbol Number:	**358**
	Symbol Explanation:	Shallow soundings, less than or equal to the safety depth
	S57/INT1	SOUNDG I 2, 4, 10-15; K 17 (I 10) OBSTRN I 2, 4; K 41, 42, 46.2; L 20, 21.2; M 43; Q 42 (L 21.2) UWTROC K 11, 12, 14.1, 14.2, 15; O 27 (K 15) WRECKS K 21, 22, 26, 27, 30 (K 30)
	Symbol Name:	SY(**SOUNDSA1**)
	Symbol Number:	**359**
	Symbol Explanation:	Symbol for drying height, used for shallow soundings, less than or equal to safety depth
	S57/INT1	UWTROC K 11 WRECKS K 21, 30 SOUNDG I 15
	Symbol Name:	SY(**SOUNDSB1**)
	Symbol Number:	**360**
	Symbol Explanation:	Symbol for swept sounding, used for shallow soundings, less than or equal to safety depth
	S57/INT1	As applicable K 2 OBSTRN K 42 WRECKS K 27
	Symbol Name:	SY(**SOUNDSC2**)
	Symbol Number:	**362**
	Symbol Explanation:	Sounding of low accuracy
	S57/INT1	As applicable B 7, 8; I 1, 3.1, 3.2 (I 1) OBSTRN I 2 SOUNDG I 2, 4, 13, 14 (I 13)
	Symbol Name:	SY(**SPRING02**)
	Symbol Number:	**363**
	Symbol Explanation:	Spring
	S57/INT1	SPRING J 15
	Symbol Name:	SY(**SWPARE51**)
	Symbol Number:	**364**
	Symbol Explanation:	Swept area
	S57/INT1	SWPARE I 24

	Symbol Name:	SY(**TIDCUR05**)
	Symbol Number:	**365**
	Symbol Explanation:	Predicted tidal stream or current direction
	S57/INT1	Non-standard object **tidcur** IEC 61174 Annex E Section 8
	Symbol Name:	SY(**TIDCUR04**)
	Symbol Number:	**366**
	Symbol Explanation:	Actual tidal stream or current direction
	S57/INT1	Non-standard object **tidcur** IEC 61174 Annex E Section 13
	Symbol Name:	SY(**TIDCUR03**)
	Symbol Number:	**367**
	Symbol Explanation:	Box for current strength
	S57/INT1	Non-standard object **tidcur** IEC 61174 Annex E Section 13
	Symbol Name:	SY(**TIDEHT01**)
	Symbol Number:	**368**
	Symbol Explanation:	Point for which tide height information is available
	S57/INT1	T_HMON not specified
		T_NHMN not specified
		T_TIMS not specified
	Symbol Name:	SY(**TIDSTR01**)
	Symbol Number:	**369**
	Symbol Explanation:	Point or area for which a tidal stream table is available
	S57/INT1	TS_PAD H 31, 46 (H 46)
		TS_PNH not specified
		TS_PRH not specified
		TS_TIS not specified
	Symbol Name:	SY(**TMARDEF1**)
	Symbol Number:	**370**
	Symbol Explanation:	Topmark for beacons, flag or other shape, paper-chart
	S57/INT1	TOPMAR Q 2-5, 9, 10, 82
	Symbol Name:	SY(**TMARDEF2**)
	Symbol Number:	**371**
	Symbol Explanation:	Topmark for buoys, flag or other shape, paper-chart
	S57/INT1	TOPMAR Q 2-5, 9, 11, 30
	Symbol Name:	SY(**TMBYRD01**)
	Symbol Number:	**372**
	Symbol Explanation:	Timber yard
	S57/INT1	PRDARE F 52
	Symbol Name:	SY(**TNKCON02**)
	Symbol Number:	**373**
	Symbol Explanation:	Tank
	S57/INT1	BUISGL Not specified
		PRDARE Not specified
		SILTNK E 32
	Symbol Name:	SY(**TNKCON12**)
	Symbol Number:	**374**
	Symbol Explanation:	Conspicuous tank
	S57/INT1	BUISGL Not specified
		PRDARE Not specified
		SILTNK E 32

	Symbol Name:	SY(**TNKFRM01**)
	Symbol Number:	**375**
	Symbol Explanation:	Tank farm
	S57/INT1	PRDARE E 32

	Symbol Name:	SY(**TNKFRM11**)
	Symbol Number:	**376**
	Symbol Explanation:	Conspicuous tank farm
	S57/INT1	PRDARE E 32

	Symbol Name:	SY(**TOPMAR02**)
	Symbol Number:	**377**
	Symbol Explanation:	Topmark for buoys, cone point up, paper-chart
	S57/INT1	TOPMAR Q 2-5, 9, 11, 30, 130.1 (Q 9)

	Symbol Name:	SY(**TOPMAR04**)
	Symbol Number:	**378**
	Symbol Explanation:	Topmark for buoys, cone point down, paper-chart
	S57/INT1	TOPMAR Not specified

	Symbol Name:	SY(**TOPMAR05**)
	Symbol Number:	**379**
	Symbol Explanation:	Topmark for buoys, 2 cones point upward, paper-chart
	S57/INT1	TOPMAR Q 2-5, 9, 11, 130.3 (Q 9)

	Symbol Name:	SY(**TOPMAR06**)
	Symbol Number:	**380**
	Symbol Explanation:	Topmark for buoys, 2 cones point downward, paper-chart
	S57/INT1	TOPMAR Q 2-5, 9, 11, 30, 130.3 (Q 9)

	Symbol Name:	SY(**TOPMAR07**)
	Symbol Number:	**381**
	Symbol Explanation:	Topmark for buoys, 2 cones base to base, paper-chart
	S57/INT1	TOPMAR Q 2-5, 9, 11, 30, 130.3 (Q 9)

	Symbol Name:	SY(**TOPMAR08**)
	Symbol Number:	**382**
	Symbol Explanation:	Topmark for buoys, 2 cones point to point, paper-chart
	S57/INT1	TOPMAR Q 2-5, 9, 11, 30, 130.3 (Q 9)

	Symbol Name:	SY(**TOPMAR10**)
	Symbol Number:	**383**
	Symbol Explanation:	Topmark for buoys, sphere, paper-chart
	S57/INT1	TOPMAR Q 2-5, 9, 11, 30, 130.5 (Q 9)

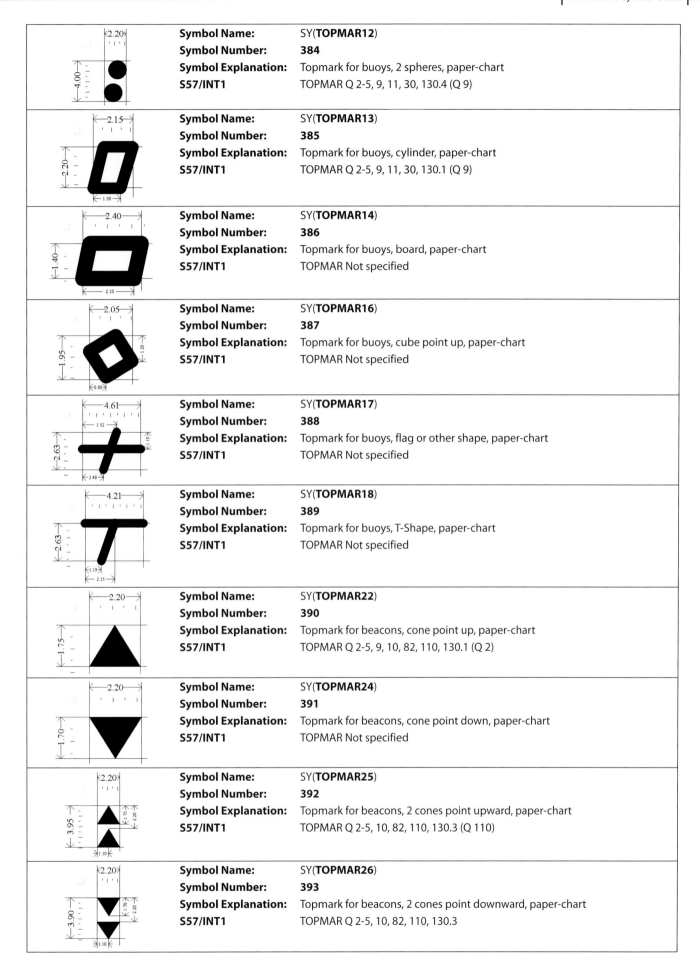

Symbol Name:	SY(**TOPMAR12**)
Symbol Number:	**384**
Symbol Explanation:	Topmark for buoys, 2 spheres, paper-chart
S57/INT1	TOPMAR Q 2-5, 9, 11, 30, 130.4 (Q 9)

Symbol Name:	SY(**TOPMAR13**)
Symbol Number:	**385**
Symbol Explanation:	Topmark for buoys, cylinder, paper-chart
S57/INT1	TOPMAR Q 2-5, 9, 11, 30, 130.1 (Q 9)

Symbol Name:	SY(**TOPMAR14**)
Symbol Number:	**386**
Symbol Explanation:	Topmark for buoys, board, paper-chart
S57/INT1	TOPMAR Not specified

Symbol Name:	SY(**TOPMAR16**)
Symbol Number:	**387**
Symbol Explanation:	Topmark for buoys, cube point up, paper-chart
S57/INT1	TOPMAR Not specified

Symbol Name:	SY(**TOPMAR17**)
Symbol Number:	**388**
Symbol Explanation:	Topmark for buoys, flag or other shape, paper-chart
S57/INT1	TOPMAR Not specified

Symbol Name:	SY(**TOPMAR18**)
Symbol Number:	**389**
Symbol Explanation:	Topmark for buoys, T-Shape, paper-chart
S57/INT1	TOPMAR Not specified

Symbol Name:	SY(**TOPMAR22**)
Symbol Number:	**390**
Symbol Explanation:	Topmark for beacons, cone point up, paper-chart
S57/INT1	TOPMAR Q 2-5, 9, 10, 82, 110, 130.1 (Q 2)

Symbol Name:	SY(**TOPMAR24**)
Symbol Number:	**391**
Symbol Explanation:	Topmark for beacons, cone point down, paper-chart
S57/INT1	TOPMAR Not specified

Symbol Name:	SY(**TOPMAR25**)
Symbol Number:	**392**
Symbol Explanation:	Topmark for beacons, 2 cones point upward, paper-chart
S57/INT1	TOPMAR Q 2-5, 10, 82, 110, 130.3 (Q 110)

Symbol Name:	SY(**TOPMAR26**)
Symbol Number:	**393**
Symbol Explanation:	Topmark for beacons, 2 cones point downward, paper-chart
S57/INT1	TOPMAR Q 2-5, 10, 82, 110, 130.3

	Symbol Name:	SY(**TOPMAR27**)
	Symbol Number:	**394**
	Symbol Explanation:	Topmark for beacons, 2 cones base to base, paper-chart
	S57/INT1	TOPMAR Q 2-5, 10, 82, 110, 130.3

	Symbol Name:	SY(**TOPMAR28**)
	Symbol Number:	**395**
	Symbol Explanation:	Topmark for beacons, 2 cones point to point, paper-chart
	S57/INT1	TOPMAR Q 2-5, 10, 82, 110, 130.3

	Symbol Name:	SY(**TOPMAR30**)
	Symbol Number:	**396**
	Symbol Explanation:	Topmark for beacons, sphere, paper-chart
	S57/INT1	TOPMAR Q 2-5, 10, 82, 110, 130.5

	Symbol Name:	SY(**TOPMAR32**)
	Symbol Number:	**397**
	Symbol Explanation:	Topmark for beacons, 2 spheres, paper-chart
	S57/INT1	TOPMAR Q 2-5, 10, 82, 110, 130.4 (Q 110)

	Symbol Name:	SY(**TOPMAR33**)
	Symbol Number:	**398**
	Symbol Explanation:	Topmark for beacons, cylinder, paper-chart
	S57/INT1	TOPMAR Q 2-5, 10, 82, 110, 130.1 (Q 110)

	Symbol Name:	SY(**TOPMAR34**)
	Symbol Number:	**399**
	Symbol Explanation:	Topmark for beacons, board, paper-chart
	S57/INT1	TOPMAR Not specified

	Symbol Name:	SY(**TOPMAR36**)
	Symbol Number:	**400**
	Symbol Explanation:	Topmark for beacons, cube point up, paper-chart
	S57/INT1	TOPMAR Q 2-5, 10, 82, 110, 123 (Q 123)

	Symbol Name:	SY(**TOPMAR65**)
	Symbol Number:	**401**
	Symbol Explanation:	Topmark for buoys, x-shape, paper-chart
	S57/INT1	TOPMAR Q 2-5, 9, 10, 50-57, 59, 62, 70, 71, 130.6 (Q 9)

	Symbol Name:	SY(**TOPMAR85**)
	Symbol Number:	**402**
	Symbol Explanation:	Topmark for beacons, x-shape, paper-chart
	S57/INT1	TOPMAR Q 2-5, 10, 82, 110, 130.6

	Symbol Name:	SY(**TOPMAR86**)
	Symbol Number:	**403**
	Symbol Explanation:	Topmark for beacons, upright cross, paper-chart
	S57/INT1	TOPMAR Q 2-5, 10, 82, 110

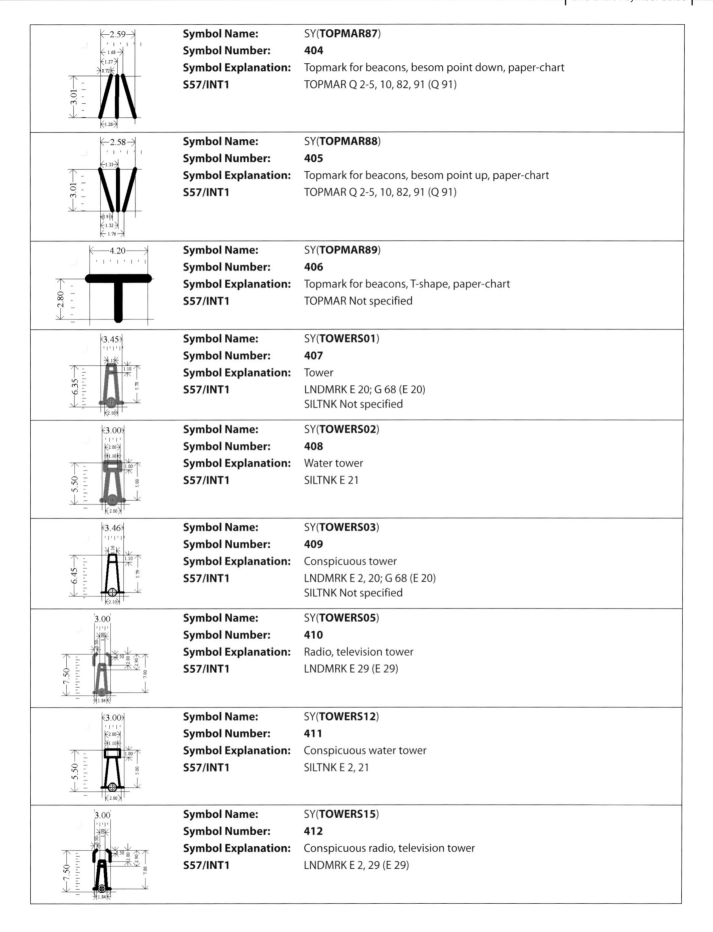

Symbol Name:	SY(**TOPMAR87**)	
Symbol Number:	**404**	
Symbol Explanation:	Topmark for beacons, besom point down, paper-chart	
S57/INT1	TOPMAR Q 2-5, 10, 82, 91 (Q 91)	

Symbol Name:	SY(**TOPMAR88**)	
Symbol Number:	**405**	
Symbol Explanation:	Topmark for beacons, besom point up, paper-chart	
S57/INT1	TOPMAR Q 2-5, 10, 82, 91 (Q 91)	

Symbol Name:	SY(**TOPMAR89**)	
Symbol Number:	**406**	
Symbol Explanation:	Topmark for beacons, T-shape, paper-chart	
S57/INT1	TOPMAR Not specified	

Symbol Name:	SY(**TOWERS01**)	
Symbol Number:	**407**	
Symbol Explanation:	Tower	
S57/INT1	LNDMRK E 20; G 68 (E 20)	
	SILTNK Not specified	

Symbol Name:	SY(**TOWERS02**)	
Symbol Number:	**408**	
Symbol Explanation:	Water tower	
S57/INT1	SILTNK E 21	

Symbol Name:	SY(**TOWERS03**)	
Symbol Number:	**409**	
Symbol Explanation:	Conspicuous tower	
S57/INT1	LNDMRK E 2, 20; G 68 (E 20)	
	SILTNK Not specified	

Symbol Name:	SY(**TOWERS05**)	
Symbol Number:	**410**	
Symbol Explanation:	Radio, television tower	
S57/INT1	LNDMRK E 29 (E 29)	

Symbol Name:	SY(**TOWERS12**)	
Symbol Number:	**411**	
Symbol Explanation:	Conspicuous water tower	
S57/INT1	SILTNK E 2, 21	

Symbol Name:	SY(**TOWERS15**)	
Symbol Number:	**412**	
Symbol Explanation:	Conspicuous radio, television tower	
S57/INT1	LNDMRK E 2, 29 (E 29)	

	Symbol Name:	SY(**TREPNT04**)
	Symbol Number:	**413**
	Symbol Explanation:	General symbol for a tree
	S57/INT1	VEGATN C 30, 31 (C 30)

	Symbol Name:	SY(**TREPNT05**)
	Symbol Number:	**414**
	Symbol Explanation:	Mangrove
	S57/INT1	VEGATN C 32

	Symbol Name:	SY(**TSLDEF51**)
	Symbol Number:	**415**
	Symbol Explanation:	One way lane of a traffic separation scheme, with the direction not defined in the data
	S57/INT1	DWRTPT M 27.1-2

	Symbol Name:	SY(**TSSCRS51**)
	Symbol Number:	**416**
	Symbol Explanation:	Traffic crossing area
	S57/INT1	TSSCRS M 23

	Symbol Name:	SY(**TSSLPT51**)
	Symbol Number:	**417**
	Symbol Explanation:	Traffic direction in a one way lane of a traffic separation scheme
	S57/INT1	DWRTPT M 27.1-2
		TSSLPT not specified

	Symbol Name:	SY(**TSSRON51**)
	Symbol Number:	**418**
	Symbol Explanation:	Traffic roundabout
	S57/INT1	TSSRON M 21

	Symbol Name:	SY(**TWRDEF51**)
	Symbol Number:	**419**
	Symbol Explanation:	Two way route of a traffic separation scheme, with the direction not defined in the data
	S57/INT1	TWRTPT M 28.2

	Symbol Name:	SY(**TWRTPT52**)
	Symbol Number:	**420**
	Symbol Explanation:	Reciprocal traffic directions in a two-way route of a traffic separation scheme
	S57/INT1	TWRTPT M 28.2

	Symbol Name:	SY(**TWRTPT53**)
	Symbol Number:	**421**
	Symbol Explanation:	Single traffic direction in a two-way route part of a traffic separation scheme
	S57/INT1	TWRTPT M 28.2

	Symbol Name:	SY(**UWTROC03**)
	Symbol Number:	**424**
	Symbol Explanation:	Dangerous underwater rock of uncertain depth
	S57/INT1	UWTROC K 13, 16 (K 13)

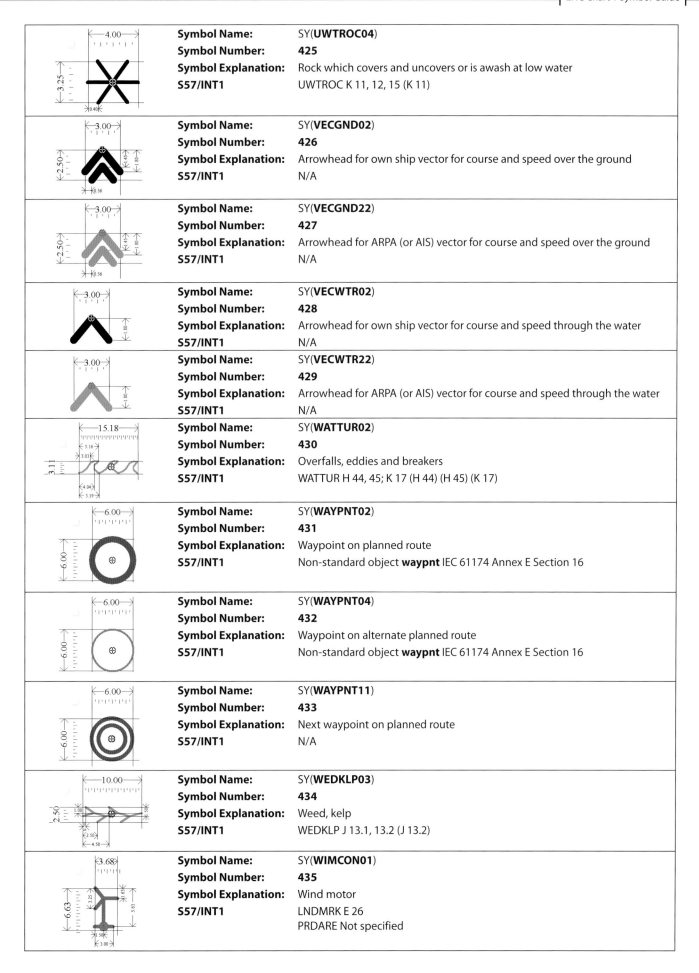

Symbol Name:	SY(**UWTROC04**)
Symbol Number:	**425**
Symbol Explanation:	Rock which covers and uncovers or is awash at low water
S57/INT1	UWTROC K 11, 12, 15 (K 11)

Symbol Name:	SY(**VECGND02**)
Symbol Number:	**426**
Symbol Explanation:	Arrowhead for own ship vector for course and speed over the ground
S57/INT1	N/A

Symbol Name:	SY(**VECGND22**)
Symbol Number:	**427**
Symbol Explanation:	Arrowhead for ARPA (or AIS) vector for course and speed over the ground
S57/INT1	N/A

Symbol Name:	SY(**VECWTR02**)
Symbol Number:	**428**
Symbol Explanation:	Arrowhead for own ship vector for course and speed through the water
S57/INT1	N/A

Symbol Name:	SY(**VECWTR22**)
Symbol Number:	**429**
Symbol Explanation:	Arrowhead for ARPA (or AIS) vector for course and speed through the water
S57/INT1	N/A

Symbol Name:	SY(**WATTUR02**)
Symbol Number:	**430**
Symbol Explanation:	Overfalls, eddies and breakers
S57/INT1	WATTUR H 44, 45; K 17 (H 44) (H 45) (K 17)

Symbol Name:	SY(**WAYPNT02**)
Symbol Number:	**431**
Symbol Explanation:	Waypoint on planned route
S57/INT1	Non-standard object **waypnt** IEC 61174 Annex E Section 16

Symbol Name:	SY(**WAYPNT04**)
Symbol Number:	**432**
Symbol Explanation:	Waypoint on alternate planned route
S57/INT1	Non-standard object **waypnt** IEC 61174 Annex E Section 16

Symbol Name:	SY(**WAYPNT11**)
Symbol Number:	**433**
Symbol Explanation:	Next waypoint on planned route
S57/INT1	N/A

Symbol Name:	SY(**WEDKLP03**)
Symbol Number:	**434**
Symbol Explanation:	Weed, kelp
S57/INT1	WEDKLP J 13.1, 13.2 (J 13.2)

Symbol Name:	SY(**WIMCON01**)
Symbol Number:	**435**
Symbol Explanation:	Wind motor
S57/INT1	LNDMRK E 26 PRDARE Not specified

Symbol Name:	SY(**WIMCON11**)
Symbol Number:	**436**
Symbol Explanation:	Conspicuous wind motor
S57/INT1	LNDMRK E 2, 26
	PRDARE Not specified

Symbol Name:	SY(**WNDFRM51**)
Symbol Number:	**437**
Symbol Explanation:	Wind generator farm
S57/INT1	PRDARE Not specified

Symbol Name:	SY(**WNDFRM61**)
Symbol Number:	**438**
Symbol Explanation:	Conspicuous wind generator farm
S57/INT1	PRDARE Not specified

Symbol Name:	SY(**WNDMIL02**)
Symbol Number:	**439**
Symbol Explanation:	Windmill
S57/INT1	LNDMRK E 25.1, 25.2 (E 25.1)

Symbol Name:	SY(**WNDMIL12**)
Symbol Number:	**440**
Symbol Explanation:	Conspicuous windmill
S57/INT1	LNDMRK E 2, 25.1, 25.2 (E 25.1)

Symbol Name:	SY(**WRECKS01**)
Symbol Number:	**441**
Symbol Explanation:	Wreck showing any portion of hull or superstructure at level of chart datum
S57/INT1	WRECKS K 20, 21, 24, 25 (K 24)

Symbol Name:	SY(**WRECKS04**)
Symbol Number:	**442**
Symbol Explanation:	Non-dangerous wreck, depth unknown
S57/INT1	WRECKS K 26, 27, 29, 30 (K 29)

Symbol Name:	SY(**WRECKS05**)
Symbol Number:	**443**
Symbol Explanation:	Dangerous wreck, depth unknown
S57/INT1	WRECKS K 22, 23, 26, 27, 28, 30 (K 28)

Symbol Name:	AP(**AIRARE02**)
Symbol Number:	**444**
Symbol Explanation:	Pattern of symbols for an airport area
S57/INT1	AIRARE D 17

Symbol Name:	AP(**DIAMOND1**)
Symbol Number:	**445**
Symbol Explanation:	Area of depth less than the safety contour
S57/INT1	N/A

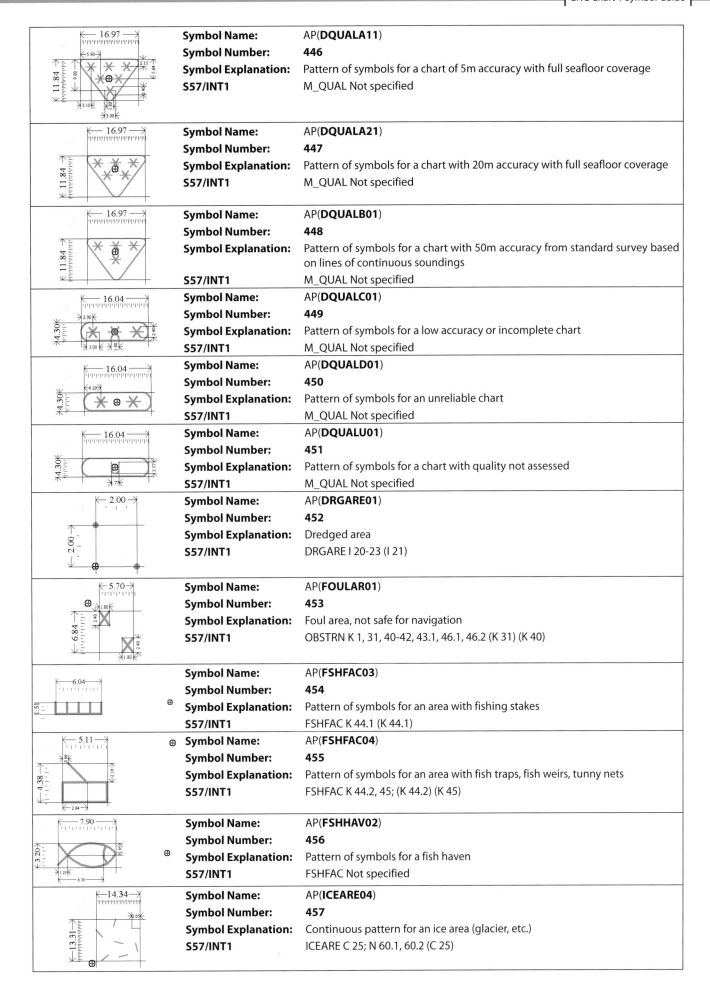

Symbol Name:	AP(**DQUALA11**)	
Symbol Number:	**446**	
Symbol Explanation:	Pattern of symbols for a chart of 5m accuracy with full seafloor coverage	
S57/INT1	M_QUAL Not specified	
Symbol Name:	AP(**DQUALA21**)	
Symbol Number:	**447**	
Symbol Explanation:	Pattern of symbols for a chart with 20m accuracy with full seafloor coverage	
S57/INT1	M_QUAL Not specified	
Symbol Name:	AP(**DQUALB01**)	
Symbol Number:	**448**	
Symbol Explanation:	Pattern of symbols for a chart with 50m accuracy from standard survey based on lines of continuous soundings	
S57/INT1	M_QUAL Not specified	
Symbol Name:	AP(**DQUALC01**)	
Symbol Number:	**449**	
Symbol Explanation:	Pattern of symbols for a low accuracy or incomplete chart	
S57/INT1	M_QUAL Not specified	
Symbol Name:	AP(**DQUALD01**)	
Symbol Number:	**450**	
Symbol Explanation:	Pattern of symbols for an unreliable chart	
S57/INT1	M_QUAL Not specified	
Symbol Name:	AP(**DQUALU01**)	
Symbol Number:	**451**	
Symbol Explanation:	Pattern of symbols for a chart with quality not assessed	
S57/INT1	M_QUAL Not specified	
Symbol Name:	AP(**DRGARE01**)	
Symbol Number:	**452**	
Symbol Explanation:	Dredged area	
S57/INT1	DRGARE I 20-23 (I 21)	
Symbol Name:	AP(**FOULAR01**)	
Symbol Number:	**453**	
Symbol Explanation:	Foul area, not safe for navigation	
S57/INT1	OBSTRN K 1, 31, 40-42, 43.1, 46.1, 46.2 (K 31) (K 40)	
Symbol Name:	AP(**FSHFAC03**)	
Symbol Number:	**454**	
Symbol Explanation:	Pattern of symbols for an area with fishing stakes	
S57/INT1	FSHFAC K 44.1 (K 44.1)	
Symbol Name:	AP(**FSHFAC04**)	
Symbol Number:	**455**	
Symbol Explanation:	Pattern of symbols for an area with fish traps, fish weirs, tunny nets	
S57/INT1	FSHFAC K 44.2, 45; (K 44.2) (K 45)	
Symbol Name:	AP(**FSHHAV02**)	
Symbol Number:	**456**	
Symbol Explanation:	Pattern of symbols for a fish haven	
S57/INT1	FSHFAC Not specified	
Symbol Name:	AP(**ICEARE04**)	
Symbol Number:	**457**	
Symbol Explanation:	Continuous pattern for an ice area (glacier, etc.)	
S57/INT1	ICEARE C 25; N 60.1, 60.2 (C 25)	

Symbol Name:	AP(**MARCUL02**)
Symbol Number:	458
Symbol Explanation:	Pattern of symbols for a marine farm
S57/INT1	MARCUL K 47, 48.1, 48.2 (K 47) (K 48.1) (K 48.2)

Symbol Name:	AP(**MARSHES1**)
Symbol Number:	459
Symbol Explanation:	Pattern of symbols for a marsh
S57/INT1	LNDRGN C 33

Symbol Name:	AP(**NODATA03**)
Symbol Number:	460
Symbol Explanation:	Area of no chart data
S57/INT1	M_QUAL Not specified
	UNSARE I 25

Symbol Name:	AP(**OVERSC01**)
Symbol Number:	461
Symbol Explanation:	Over scale part of a display containing data from more than one navigation purpose
S57/INT1	M_CSCL Not specified

Symbol Name:	AP(**PRTSUR01**)
Symbol Number:	462
Symbol Explanation:	Incompletely surveyed area
S57/INT1	DEPARE Not specified

Symbol Name:	AP(**QUESMRK1**)
Symbol Number:	463
Symbol Explanation:	Pattern of symbols for an area which is not sufficiently described to be symbolized, or for which no symbol exists in the symbol library
S57/INT1	N/A

Symbol Name:	AP(**RCKLDG01**)
Symbol Number:	464
Symbol Explanation:	Rock or coral drying ledges
S57/INT1	SBDARE J 9, 10, 21, 22, 38 (J 22)

Symbol Name:	AP(**SNDWAV01**)
Symbol Number:	465
Symbol Explanation:	Pattern of symbols for sand waves
S57/INT1	SNDWAV J 14

Symbol Name:	AP(**TSSJCT02**)
Symbol Number:	466
Symbol Explanation:	Precautionary area or a traffic separation scheme crossing or roundabout
S57/INT1	PRCARE M 16, 24 (M 16)
	TSSCRS M 23
	TSSLPT M 10
	TSSRON M 21

Symbol Name:	AP(**VEGATN03**)
Symbol Number:	467
Symbol Explanation:	Pattern of symbols for wooded areas
S57/INT1	VEGATN C 14, 30, 31.1-31.8; G 37-39 (C 30) (C 31.4)

Symbol Name:	AP(**VEGATN04**)
Symbol Number:	468
Symbol Explanation:	Pattern of symbols for mangroves
S57/INT1	VEGATN C 32

	Symbol Name:	LC(**ACHARE51**)
	Symbol Number:	**469**
	Symbol Explanation:	Boundary of an anchorage area
	S57/INT1	ACHARE N 12.1-9; (N 12.1)

	Symbol Name:	LC(**ACHRES51**)
	Symbol Number:	**470**
	Symbol Explanation:	Boundary of an area where anchoring is prohibited or restricted
	S57/INT1	RESARE N 20

	Symbol Name:	LC(**ADMARE01**)
	Symbol Number:	**471**
	Symbol Explanation:	Jurisdiction boundary
	S57/INT1	N/A

	Symbol Name:	LC(**CBLARE51**)
	Symbol Number:	**472**
	Symbol Explanation:	Boundary of a submarine cable area
	S57/INT1	CBLARE L 30.2, 31.2; (L 30.2) (L 31.2)

	Symbol Name:	LC(**CBLSUB06**)
	Symbol Number:	**473**
	Symbol Explanation:	Submarine cable
	S57/INT1	CBLSUB L 30.1, 31.1, 32 (L 30.1) (L 31.1) (L 32)

	Symbol Name:	LC(**CHCRDEL1**)
	Symbol Number:	**474**
	Symbol Explanation:	This line has been deleted by a manual update
	S57/INT1	N/A

	Symbol Name:	LC(**CHCRID01**)
	Symbol Number:	**475**
	Symbol Explanation:	This line has been manually updated
	S57/INT1	N/A

	Symbol Name:	LC(**CTNARE51**)
	Symbol Number:	**476**
	Symbol Explanation:	Boundary of area with a specific caution
	S57/INT1	CTNARE N 1.1, 1.2 (N 1.2)
		TSSLPT not specified

	Symbol Name:	LC(**CTYARE51**)
	Symbol Number:	**477**
	Symbol Explanation:	Boundary of area to be navigated with caution
	S57/INT1	CTSARE N 64
		DMPGRD N 23-24, 62.1-2 (N 23.1)
		ICNARE N 65
		MIPARE N 30, 32, 33 (N 32)
		OSPARE L 1, 4
		PILBOP T 1.1 - 1.4
		RESARE N 2.1, 2.2, 34, 63
		SPLARE N 13
		SUBTLN N 33
		TWRTPT M 28.2

	Symbol Name:	LC(**DWLDEF01**)
	Symbol Number:	**478**
	Symbol Explanation:	Deep water route centreline, direction not defined in the data
	S57/INT1	DWRTCL M 27.3

	Symbol Name:	LC(**DWRTCL05**)
	Symbol Number:	**479**
	Symbol Explanation:	Two-way deep water route centreline, not based on fixed marks
	S57/INT1	DWRTCL M 27.3

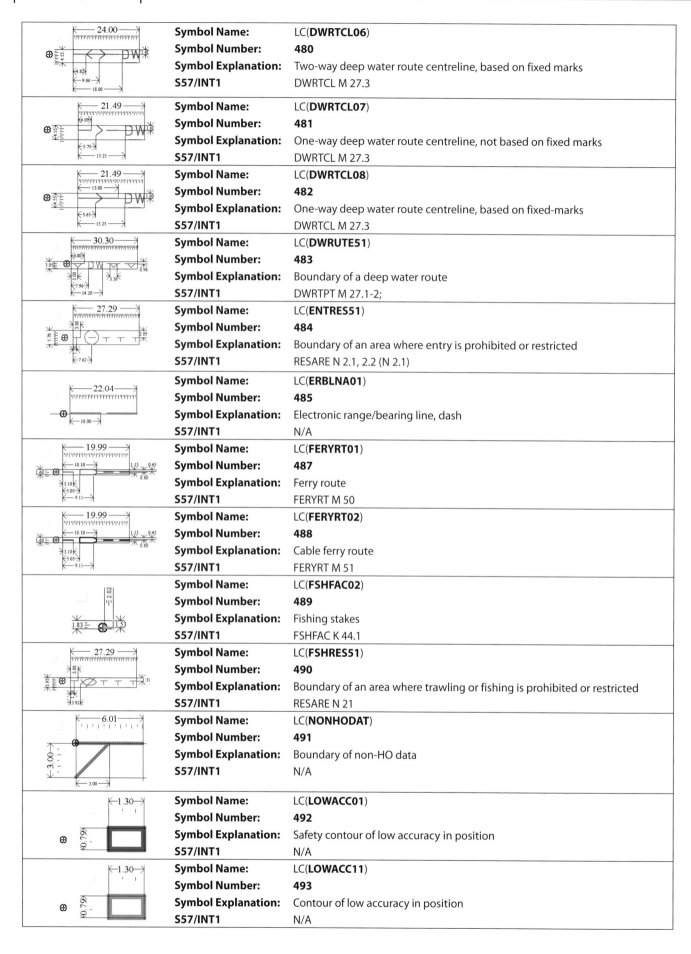

Symbol Name:	LC(**DWRTCL06**)	
Symbol Number:	**480**	
Symbol Explanation:	Two-way deep water route centreline, based on fixed marks	
S57/INT1	DWRTCL M 27.3	
Symbol Name:	LC(**DWRTCL07**)	
Symbol Number:	**481**	
Symbol Explanation:	One-way deep water route centreline, not based on fixed marks	
S57/INT1	DWRTCL M 27.3	
Symbol Name:	LC(**DWRTCL08**)	
Symbol Number:	**482**	
Symbol Explanation:	One-way deep water route centreline, based on fixed-marks	
S57/INT1	DWRTCL M 27.3	
Symbol Name:	LC(**DWRUTE51**)	
Symbol Number:	**483**	
Symbol Explanation:	Boundary of a deep water route	
S57/INT1	DWRTPT M 27.1-2;	
Symbol Name:	LC(**ENTRES51**)	
Symbol Number:	**484**	
Symbol Explanation:	Boundary of an area where entry is prohibited or restricted	
S57/INT1	RESARE N 2.1, 2.2 (N 2.1)	
Symbol Name:	LC(**ERBLNA01**)	
Symbol Number:	**485**	
Symbol Explanation:	Electronic range/bearing line, dash	
S57/INT1	N/A	
Symbol Name:	LC(**FERYRT01**)	
Symbol Number:	**487**	
Symbol Explanation:	Ferry route	
S57/INT1	FERYRT M 50	
Symbol Name:	LC(**FERYRT02**)	
Symbol Number:	**488**	
Symbol Explanation:	Cable ferry route	
S57/INT1	FERYRT M 51	
Symbol Name:	LC(**FSHFAC02**)	
Symbol Number:	**489**	
Symbol Explanation:	Fishing stakes	
S57/INT1	FSHFAC K 44.1	
Symbol Name:	LC(**FSHRES51**)	
Symbol Number:	**490**	
Symbol Explanation:	Boundary of an area where trawling or fishing is prohibited or restricted	
S57/INT1	RESARE N 21	
Symbol Name:	LC(**NONHODAT**)	
Symbol Number:	**491**	
Symbol Explanation:	Boundary of non-HO data	
S57/INT1	N/A	
Symbol Name:	LC(**LOWACC01**)	
Symbol Number:	**492**	
Symbol Explanation:	Safety contour of low accuracy in position	
S57/INT1	N/A	
Symbol Name:	LC(**LOWACC11**)	
Symbol Number:	**493**	
Symbol Explanation:	Contour of low accuracy in position	
S57/INT1	N/A	

	Symbol Name:	LC(**LOWACC21**)
	Symbol Number:	**494**
	Symbol Explanation:	Coastline or shoreline construction of low accuracy in position
	S57/INT1	SLCONS F 30,31; O 89 (F 31)
		COALNE C 2, 32, 33; O 89 (C 2)

	Symbol Name:	LC(**LOWACC31**)
	Symbol Number:	**495**
	Symbol Explanation:	Area of wrecks or obstructions of low accuracy
	S57/INT1	OBSTRN Not specified

	Symbol Name:	LC(**LOWACC41**)
	Symbol Number:	**496**
	Symbol Explanation:	Danger line of low accuracy surrounding a foul area
	S57/INT1	OBSTRN I 3.1, 3.2; O 89
		WRECKS I 3.1, 3.2; O 89

	Symbol Name:	LC(**MARSYS51**)
	Symbol Number:	**497**
	Symbol Explanation:	Boundary between IALA-A and IALA-B systems of lateral buoys and beacons
	S57/INT1	M_NSYS Q 130.1

	Symbol Name:	LC(**NAVARE51**)
	Symbol Number:	**498**
	Symbol Explanation:	Boundary of a navigation feature such as a fairway, magnetic anomaly, etc.
	S57/INT1	FAIRWY not specified;
		FERYRT M 50, 51;
		FSHFAC K 44.1-2, 45;
		HRBARE N 49;
		LOCMAG B 82.1-2; (B 82.1)
		MARCUL K 47, 48.1 - 2;
		M_NSYS Q 130-130.6;
		OBSTRN K 1, 31, 40-43, 46.1-2; L 21, 23; Q .42;
		RECTRC M 1, 3-4, 5.1, 5.2, 6;
		SNDWAV J 14;
		SWPARE I 24;
		WRECKS K 20-30;

	Symbol Name:	LC(**PIPARE51**)
	Symbol Number:	**499**
	Symbol Explanation:	Boundary of a submarine pipeline area with potentially dangerous contents
	S57/INT1	PIPARE L 40.2, 41.2 (L 40.2)

	Symbol Name:	LC(**PIPARE61**)
	Symbol Number:	**500**
	Symbol Explanation:	Boundary of a submarine pipeline area with generally non-dangerous contents
	S57/INT1	PIPARE L 40.2, 41.2; (L 41.2)

	Symbol Name:	LC(**PIPSOL05**)
	Symbol Number:	**501**
	Symbol Explanation:	Oil, gas pipeline, submerged or on land
	S57/INT1	PIPSOL D 29; L 42, 44 (D 29) (L 42) (L 44)

	Symbol Name:	LC(**PIPSOL06**)
	Symbol Number:	**502**
	Symbol Explanation:	Water pipeline, sewer, etc.
	S57/INT1	PIPSOL L 41.1

	Symbol Name:	LC(**PLNRTE04**)
	Symbol Number:	**503**
	Symbol Explanation:	Planned route for own ship
	S57/INT1	N/A

	Symbol Name:	LC(**PRCARE51**)
	Symbol Number:	**504**
	Symbol Explanation:	Boundary of a precautionary area
	S57/INT1	PRCARE M 16, 24;

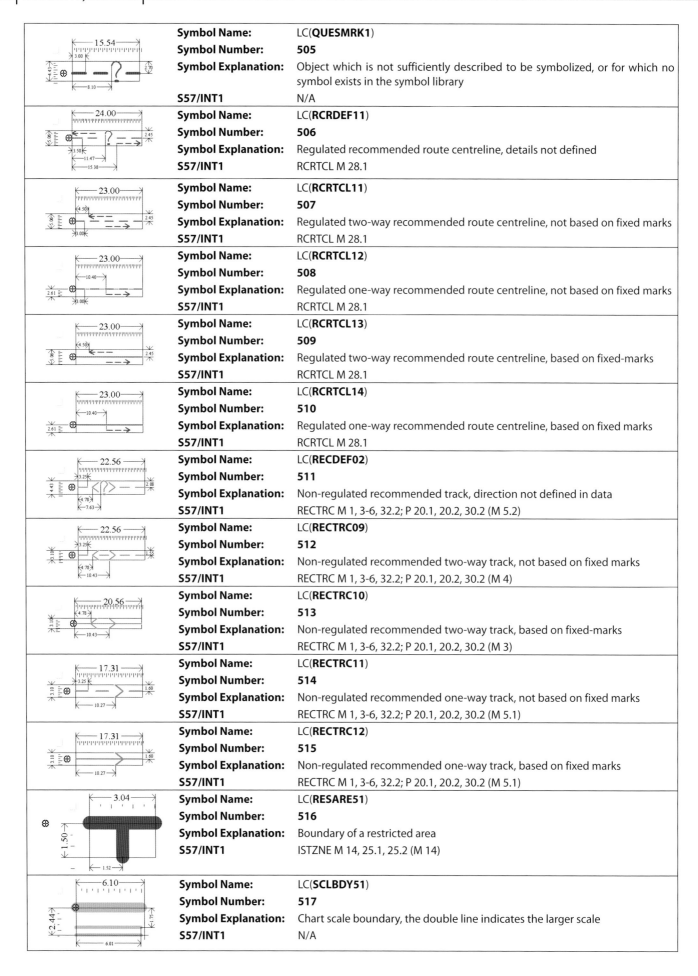

	Symbol Name:	LC(**QUESMRK1**)
	Symbol Number:	505
	Symbol Explanation:	Object which is not sufficiently described to be symbolized, or for which no symbol exists in the symbol library
	S57/INT1	N/A
	Symbol Name:	LC(**RCRDEF11**)
	Symbol Number:	506
	Symbol Explanation:	Regulated recommended route centreline, details not defined
	S57/INT1	RCRTCL M 28.1
	Symbol Name:	LC(**RCRTCL11**)
	Symbol Number:	507
	Symbol Explanation:	Regulated two-way recommended route centreline, not based on fixed marks
	S57/INT1	RCRTCL M 28.1
	Symbol Name:	LC(**RCRTCL12**)
	Symbol Number:	508
	Symbol Explanation:	Regulated one-way recommended route centreline, not based on fixed marks
	S57/INT1	RCRTCL M 28.1
	Symbol Name:	LC(**RCRTCL13**)
	Symbol Number:	509
	Symbol Explanation:	Regulated two-way recommended route centreline, based on fixed-marks
	S57/INT1	RCRTCL M 28.1
	Symbol Name:	LC(**RCRTCL14**)
	Symbol Number:	510
	Symbol Explanation:	Regulated one-way recommended route centreline, based on fixed marks
	S57/INT1	RCRTCL M 28.1
	Symbol Name:	LC(**RECDEF02**)
	Symbol Number:	511
	Symbol Explanation:	Non-regulated recommended track, direction not defined in data
	S57/INT1	RECTRC M 1, 3-6, 32.2; P 20.1, 20.2, 30.2 (M 5.2)
	Symbol Name:	LC(**RECTRC09**)
	Symbol Number:	512
	Symbol Explanation:	Non-regulated recommended two-way track, not based on fixed marks
	S57/INT1	RECTRC M 1, 3-6, 32.2; P 20.1, 20.2, 30.2 (M 4)
	Symbol Name:	LC(**RECTRC10**)
	Symbol Number:	513
	Symbol Explanation:	Non-regulated recommended two-way track, based on fixed-marks
	S57/INT1	RECTRC M 1, 3-6, 32.2; P 20.1, 20.2, 30.2 (M 3)
	Symbol Name:	LC(**RECTRC11**)
	Symbol Number:	514
	Symbol Explanation:	Non-regulated recommended one-way track, not based on fixed marks
	S57/INT1	RECTRC M 1, 3-6, 32.2; P 20.1, 20.2, 30.2 (M 5.1)
	Symbol Name:	LC(**RECTRC12**)
	Symbol Number:	515
	Symbol Explanation:	Non-regulated recommended one-way track, based on fixed marks
	S57/INT1	RECTRC M 1, 3-6, 32.2; P 20.1, 20.2, 30.2 (M 5.1)
	Symbol Name:	LC(**RESARE51**)
	Symbol Number:	516
	Symbol Explanation:	Boundary of a restricted area
	S57/INT1	ISTZNE M 14, 25.1, 25.2 (M 14)
	Symbol Name:	LC(**SCLBDY51**)
	Symbol Number:	517
	Symbol Explanation:	Chart scale boundary, the double line indicates the larger scale
	S57/INT1	N/A

	Symbol Name:	LC(**TIDINF51**)
	Symbol Number:	**518**
	Symbol Explanation:	Boundary of an area for which there is tidal information
	S57/INT1	TS_FEB H 40-41
		TS_PAD H 31
		TS_PNH Not specified
		TS_PRH Not specified
		TS_TIS Not specified
		T_HMON Not specified
		T_NHMN Not specified
		T_TIMS Not specified

	Symbol Name:	SY(**PSSARE01**)
	Symbol Number:	**519**
	Symbol Explanation:	PSSA - centred symbol
	S57/INT1	RESARE, CATREA 28, N22

	Symbol Name:	LC(**ARCSLN01**)
	Symbol Number:	**520**
	Symbol Explanation:	Boundary of archipelago sea lane
	S57/INT1	ARCSLN M17

	Symbol Name:	SY(**DIRBOY01**)
	Symbol Number:	**521**
	Symbol Explanation:	Direction of buoyage
	S57/INT1	M_NSYS Q 130.1, 130.2 (Q 130.2)

	Symbol Name:	SY(**DWRUTE51**)
	Symbol Number:	**522**
	Symbol Explanation:	Reciprocal traffic directions in a two-way part of a deep-water route
	S57/INT1	DWRTPT M 27.1-2

	Symbol Name:	SY(**BLKADJ01**)
	Symbol Number:	**523**
	Symbol Explanation:	Symbol to be used for checking and adjusting the brightness and contrast controls
	S57/INT1	N/A

	Symbol Name:	SY(**FLTHAZ02**)
	Symbol Number:	**524**
	Symbol Explanation:	Floating hazard to navigation
	S57/INT1	LOGPON N 61
		OBSTRN G 178

	Symbol Name:	SY(**DANGER03**)
	Symbol Number:	**525**
	Symbol Explanation:	Underwater hazard which covers and uncovers
	S57/INT1	UWTROC K 11, 12 (K 11)

	Symbol Name:	SY(**OBSTRN03**)
	Symbol Number:	**526**
	Symbol Explanation:	Obstruction which covers and uncovers
	S57/INT1	OBSTRN K 1

	Symbol Name:	SY(**BOYSPP35**)
	Symbol Number:	**527**
	Symbol Explanation:	Special purpose ice buoy or spar or pillar shaped buoy, simplified
	S57/INT1	BOYSPP Q 130.6

	Symbol Name:	SY(**SAFCON00**)
	Symbol Number:	**528**
	Symbol Explanation:	Contour label
	S57/INT1	DEPARE not specified
		DEPCNT I 30, 31 (I 30)
		DRGARE not specified

	Symbol Name:	SY(**SAFCON01**)
	Symbol Number:	**529**
	Symbol Explanation:	Contour label
	S57/INT1	DEPARE not specified
		DEPCNT I 30, 31 (I 30)
		DRGARE not specified

	Symbol Name:	SY(**SAFCON02**)
	Symbol Number:	**530**
	Symbol Explanation:	Contour label
	S57/INT1	DEPARE not specified
		DEPCNT I 30, 31 (I 30)
		DRGARE not specified

	Symbol Name:	SY(**SAFCON03**)
	Symbol Number:	**531**
	Symbol Explanation:	Contour label
	S57/INT1	DEPARE not specified
		DEPCNT I 30, 31 (I 30)
		DRGARE not specified

	Symbol Name:	SY(**SAFCON04**)
	Symbol Number:	**532**
	Symbol Explanation:	Contour label
	S57/INT1	DEPARE not specified
		DEPCNT I 30, 31 (I 30)
		DRGARE not specified

	Symbol Name:	SY(**SAFCON05**)
	Symbol Number:	**533**
	Symbol Explanation:	Contour label
	S57/INT1	DEPARE not specified
		DEPCNT I 30, 31 (I 30)
		DRGARE not specified

	Symbol Name:	SY(**SAFCON06**)
	Symbol Number:	**534**
	Symbol Explanation:	Contour label
	S57/INT1	DEPARE not specified
		DEPCNT I 30, 31 (I 30)
		DRGARE not specified

	Symbol Name:	SY(**SAFCON07**)
	Symbol Number:	**535**
	Symbol Explanation:	Contour label
	S57/INT1	DEPARE not specified
		DEPCNT I 30, 31 (I 30)
		DRGARE not specified

	Symbol Name:	SY(**SAFCON08**)
	Symbol Number:	**536**
	Symbol Explanation:	Contour label
	S57/INT1	DEPARE not specified
		DEPCNT I 30, 31 (I 30)
		DRGARE not specified

	Symbol Name:	SY(**SAFCON09**)
	Symbol Number:	**537**
	Symbol Explanation:	Contour label
	S57/INT1	DEPARE not specified
		DEPCNT I 30, 31 (I 30)
		DRGARE not specified
	Symbol Name:	SY(**SAFCON10**)
	Symbol Number:	**538**
	Symbol Explanation:	Contour label
	S57/INT1	DEPARE not specified
		DEPCNT I 30, 31 (I 30)
		DRGARE not specified
	Symbol Name:	SY(**SAFCON11**)
	Symbol Number:	**539**
	Symbol Explanation:	Contour label
	S57/INT1	DEPARE not specified
		DEPCNT I 30, 31 (I 30)
		DRGARE not specified
	Symbol Name:	SY(**SAFCON12**)
	Symbol Number:	**540**
	Symbol Explanation:	Contour label
	S57/INT1	DEPARE not specified
		DEPCNT I 30, 31 (I 30)
		DRGARE not specified
	Symbol Name:	SY(**SAFCON13**)
	Symbol Number:	**541**
	Symbol Explanation:	Contour label
	S57/INT1	DEPARE not specified
		DEPCNT I 30, 31 (I 30)
		DRGARE not specified
	Symbol Name:	SY(**SAFCON14**)
	Symbol Number:	**542**
	Symbol Explanation:	Contour label
	S57/INT1	DEPARE not specified
		DEPCNT I 30, 31 (I 30)
		DRGARE not specified
	Symbol Name:	SY(**SAFCON15**)
	Symbol Number:	**543**
	Symbol Explanation:	Contour label
	S57/INT1	DEPARE not specified
		DEPCNT I 30, 31 (I 30)
		DRGARE not specified
	Symbol Name:	SY(**SAFCON16**)
	Symbol Number:	**544**
	Symbol Explanation:	Contour label
	S57/INT1	DEPARE not specified
		DEPCNT I 30, 31 (I 30)
		DRGARE not specified
	Symbol Name:	SY(**SAFCON17**)
	Symbol Number:	**545**
	Symbol Explanation:	Contour label
	S57/INT1	DEPARE not specified
		DEPCNT I 30, 31 (I 30)
		DRGARE not specified
	Symbol Name:	SY(**SAFCON18**)
	Symbol Number:	**546**
	Symbol Explanation:	Contour label
	S57/INT1	DEPARE not specified
		DEPCNT I 30, 31 (I 30)
		DRGARE not specified

	Symbol Name:	SY(**SAFCON19**)
	Symbol Number:	**547**
	Symbol Explanation:	Contour label
	S57/INT1	DEPARE not specified
		DEPCNT I 30, 31 (I 30)
		DRGARE not specified
	Symbol Name:	SY(**SAFCON20**)
	Symbol Number:	**548**
	Symbol Explanation:	Contour label
	S57/INT1	DEPARE not specified
		DEPCNT I 30, 31 (I 30)
		DRGARE not specified
	Symbol Name:	SY(**SAFCON21**)
	Symbol Number:	**549**
	Symbol Explanation:	Contour label
	S57/INT1	DEPARE not specified
		DEPCNT I 30, 31 (I 30)
		DRGARE not specified
	Symbol Name:	SY(**SAFCON22**)
	Symbol Number:	**550**
	Symbol Explanation:	Contour label
	S57/INT1	DEPARE not specified
		DEPCNT I 30, 31 (I 30)
		DRGARE not specified
	Symbol Name:	SY(**SAFCON23**)
	Symbol Number:	**551**
	Symbol Explanation:	Contour label
	S57/INT1	DEPARE not specified
		DEPCNT I 30, 31 (I 30)
		DRGARE not specified
	Symbol Name:	SY(**SAFCON24**)
	Symbol Number:	**552**
	Symbol Explanation:	Contour label
	S57/INT1	DEPARE not specified
		DEPCNT I 30, 31 (I 30)
		DRGARE not specified
	Symbol Name:	SY(**SAFCON25**)
	Symbol Number:	**553**
	Symbol Explanation:	Contour label
	S57/INT1	DEPARE not specified
		DEPCNT I 30, 31 (I 30)
		DRGARE not specified
	Symbol Name:	SY(**SAFCON26**)
	Symbol Number:	**554**
	Symbol Explanation:	Contour label
	S57/INT1	DEPARE not specified
		DEPCNT I 30, 31 (I 30)
		DRGARE not specified
	Symbol Name:	SY(**SAFCON27**)
	Symbol Number:	**555**
	Symbol Explanation:	Contour label
	S57/INT1	DEPARE not specified
		DEPCNT I 30, 31 (I 30)
		DRGARE not specified
	Symbol Name:	SY(**SAFCON28**)
	Symbol Number:	**556**
	Symbol Explanation:	Contour label
	S57/INT1	DEPARE not specified
		DEPCNT I 30, 31 (I 30)
		DRGARE not specified

	Symbol Name:	SY(**SAFCON29**)
	Symbol Number:	**557**
	Symbol Explanation:	Contour label
	S57/INT1	DEPARE not specified
		DEPCNT I 30, 31 (I 30)
		DRGARE not specified

	Symbol Name:	SY(**SAFCON50**)
	Symbol Number:	**558**
	Symbol Explanation:	Contour label
	S57/INT1	DEPARE not specified
		DEPCNT I 30, 31 (I 30)
		DRGARE not specified

	Symbol Name:	SY(**SAFCON51**)
	Symbol Number:	**559**
	Symbol Explanation:	Contour label
	S57/INT1	DEPARE not specified
		DEPCNT I 30, 31 (I 30)
		DRGARE not specified

	Symbol Name:	SY(**SAFCON52**)
	Symbol Number:	**560**
	Symbol Explanation:	Contour label
	S57/INT1	DEPARE not specified
		DEPCNT I 30, 31 (I 30)
		DRGARE not specified

	Symbol Name:	SY(**SAFCON53**)
	Symbol Number:	**561**
	Symbol Explanation:	Contour label
	S57/INT1	DEPARE not specified
		DEPCNT I 30, 31 (I 30)
		DRGARE not specified

	Symbol Name:	SY(**SAFCON54**)
	Symbol Number:	**562**
	Symbol Explanation:	Contour label
	S57/INT1	DEPARE not specified
		DEPCNT I 30, 31 (I 30)
		DRGARE not specified

	Symbol Name:	SY(**SAFCON55**)
	Symbol Number:	**563**
	Symbol Explanation:	Contour label
	S57/INT1	DEPARE not specified
		DEPCNT I 30, 31 (I 30)
		DRGARE not specified

	Symbol Name:	SY(**SAFCON56**)
	Symbol Number:	**564**
	Symbol Explanation:	Contour label
	S57/INT1	DEPARE not specified
		DEPCNT I 30, 31 (I 30)
		DRGARE not specified

	Symbol Name:	SY(**SAFCON57**)
	Symbol Number:	**565**
	Symbol Explanation:	Contour label
	S57/INT1	DEPARE not specified
		DEPCNT I 30, 31 (I 30)
		DRGARE not specified

	Symbol Name:	SY(**SAFCON58**)
	Symbol Number:	**566**
	Symbol Explanation:	Contour label
	S57/INT1	DEPARE not specified
		DEPCNT I 30, 31 (I 30)
		DRGARE not specified

	Symbol Name:	SY(**SAFCON59**)
	Symbol Number:	**567**
	Symbol Explanation:	Contour label
	S57/INT1	DEPARE not specified DEPCNT I 30, 31 (I 30) DRGARE not specified
	Symbol Name:	SY(**SAFCON60**)
	Symbol Number:	**568**
	Symbol Explanation:	Contour label
	S57/INT1	DEPARE not specified DEPCNT I 30, 31 (I 30) DRGARE not specified
	Symbol Name:	SY(**SAFCON61**)
	Symbol Number:	**569**
	Symbol Explanation:	Contour label
	S57/INT1	DEPARE not specified DEPCNT I 30, 31 (I 30) DRGARE not specified
	Symbol Name:	SY(**SAFCON62**)
	Symbol Number:	**570**
	Symbol Explanation:	Contour label
	S57/INT1	DEPARE not specified DEPCNT I 30, 31 (I 30) DRGARE not specified
	Symbol Name:	SY(**SAFCON63**)
	Symbol Number:	**571**
	Symbol Explanation:	Contour label
	S57/INT1	DEPARE not specified DEPCNT I 30, 31 (I 30) DRGARE not specified
	Symbol Name:	SY(**SAFCON64**)
	Symbol Number:	**572**
	Symbol Explanation:	Contour label
	S57/INT1	DEPARE not specified DEPCNT I 30, 31 (I 30) DRGARE not specified
	Symbol Name:	SY(**SAFCON65**)
	Symbol Number:	**573**
	Symbol Explanation:	Contour label
	S57/INT1	DEPARE not specified DEPCNT I 30, 31 (I 30) DRGARE not specified
	Symbol Name:	SY(**SAFCON66**)
	Symbol Number:	**574**
	Symbol Explanation:	Contour label
	S57/INT1	DEPARE not specified DEPCNT I 30, 31 (I 30) DRGARE not specified
	Symbol Name:	SY(**SAFCON67**)
	Symbol Number:	**575**
	Symbol Explanation:	Contour label
	S57/INT1	DEPARE not specified DEPCNT I 30, 31 (I 30) DRGARE not specified
	Symbol Name:	SY(**SAFCON68**)
	Symbol Number:	**576**
	Symbol Explanation:	Contour label
	S57/INT1	DEPARE not specified DEPCNT I 30, 31 (I 30) DRGARE not specified

	Symbol Name:	SY(**SAFCON69**)
	Symbol Number:	**577**
	Symbol Explanation:	Contour label
	S57/INT1	DEPARE not specified
		DEPCNT I 30, 31 (I 30)
		DRGARE not specified
	Symbol Name:	SY(**NEWOBJ01**)
	Symbol Number:	**578**
	Symbol Explanation:	New object
	S57/INT1	NEWOBJ N/A
	Symbol Name:	SY(**AISDGR02**)
	Symbol Number:	**579**
	Symbol Explanation:	Dangerous AIS target
	S57/INT1:	N/A
	Symbol Name:	SY(**AISLST02**)
	Symbol Number:	**580**
	Symbol Explanation:	Lost AIS target
	S57/INT1:	N/A S 17
	Symbol Name:	SY(**AISTRN03**)
	Symbol Number:	**582**
	Symbol Explanation:	AIS target turning to starboard
	S57/INT1:	N/A
	Symbol Name:	SY(**AISTRN04**)
	Symbol Number:	**583**
	Symbol Explanation:	AIS target turning to port
	S57/INT1:	N/A
	Symbol Name:	LC(**NEWOBJ01**)
	Symbol Number:	**584**
	Symbol Explanation:	New object
	S57/INT1	NEWOBJ N/A
	Symbol Name:	SY(**ESSARE01**)
	Symbol Number:	**585**
	Symbol Explanation:	ESSA - centred symbol
	S57/INT1	RESARE,
		CATREA 27 N22
	Symbol Name:	LC(**ESSARE01**)
	Symbol Number:	**586**
	Symbol Explanation:	Boundary of an ESSA or PSSA
	S57/INT1	RESARE,
		CATREA 27 or 28 N 22
	Symbol Name:	SY(**DRFSTA01**)
	Symbol Number:	**587**
	Symbol Explanation:	DGPS reference station
	S57/INT1:	RDOSTA S 51 (S 10)
	Symbol Name:	SY(**AISATN02**)
	Symbol Number:	**588**
	Symbol Explanation:	AIS based aid to navigation
	S57/INT1:	N/A

Symbol Name:	SY(**AISTSO01**)
Symbol Number:	**589**
Symbol Explanation:	AIS target – true scale outline
S57/INT1:	N/A

81